THE RULE

Of

St. Benedict

With Explanatory Notes

Saint Benedict

BIBLIOGRAPHIC INFORMATION

This reprint edition of *The Rule of St. Benedict* was previously translated from the Latin into English by D. Oswald Hunter Blair, M.A., Monk of Fort-Augustus and published at the Abbey Press in London in 1906. The 1906 publication contained the Latin text but has been removed from this reprint edition. Spelling, grammar, punctuation, and wording have been gently updated.

an Ichthus Publications *edition*

www.ichthuspublications.com

CONTENTS

PREFACE

MORE THAN THIRTEEN HUNDRED years have passed away since the founder and father of western monachism gave to the world, from the solitude of Monte Cassino,* the code of religious life which the consensus of Christian centuries has stamped with the distinctive title of the *Holy Rule.*

Forming as it did for so many ages one of the most powerful instruments of the civilization of Europe, the *Rule of St. Benedict* possesses—apart from its intrinsic merits, or its value as a literary monument of the early Church—an interest which is not limited to the Benedictine family alone, but which cannot but be shared by every thoughtful student of history.

The English version here presented, which has been undertaken in compliance with the demand for a new translation of the Holy Rule, will be found, it is hoped, to have at least the merit of faithfully rendering the original text. It has been the translator's aim, at the same time, to preserve as far as possible the simplicity of style which, next to the supernatural wisdom that illuminates every page, is perhaps the most striking characteristic of the Holy Rule.

The Latin text adopted, which will be found to differ slightly from that of recent English editions, was first printed in 1659 by D. Augustine de Ferrariis, a monk of Monte Cassino, from the most ancient and authentic manuscripts in the archives of that venerable monastery. The text in question (since reprinted in the *Florilegium Bibliothecæ Casinensis*) has been carefully collated throughout with a manuscript copy of the Rule, and commentary of Bernard of M. Cassino, dating from the 13th century, and in the possession of Fort-Augustus Abbey. Variations of any special interest are noted in the margin.

The *Dates* in small type indicate the portion of the Holy Rule appointed to be read daily in monasteries, usually at the end of Prime.

---

* About 535 A.D.

The explanatory notes are chiefly based upon the most ancient and approved commentaries on the Holy Rule; and it is hoped that they will be found of service in the elucidation of various passages whose meaning is not apparent from a mere verbal rendering of the original text. It has been thought best to place the notes in an appendix, rather than at the foot of the page, in order not to interfere with the use of the Holy Rule for purposes of devotion or meditation, for which it is so admirably adapted.

May this little work go forth bearing with it the blessing of our dear Holy Father Saint Benedict; and may it be the means, under God, of making his name more widely known, and more abundantly honored, in the land that was once his by a hundred ties.

ST. BENEDICT'S ABBEY,
FORT-AUGUSTUS, N.B.
Solemnity of our most Holy Father St. Benedict, 1886

Note to Second Edition.

The text of the *Rule,* as well as the translation and notes, have been carefully revised throughout; and the editor desires to express his gratitude to kind friends and critics—both within and without the Benedictine family—who have helped him with suggestions and emendations.

As the scope of this little book is devotional rather than critical, it has been thought unnecessary to reprint the few variations in the Latin text which were given as marginal notes in the former edition.

D. O. H. B.

Oxford, 1906

PROLOGUE

of Our Most Holy Father St. Benedict to his Rule

HEARKEN, O MY SON, to the precepts of thy Master, and incline the ear of thine heart; willingly receive and faithfully fulfill the admonition of thy loving Father, that thou
mayest return by the labor of obedience to Him from whom thou hadst departed through the sloth of disobedience. To thee, therefore, my words are now addressed, whoever thou art that, renouncing thine own will, dost take up the strong and bright weapons of obedience, in order to fight for the LORD Christ, our true king. In the first place, whatever good work thou beginnest to do, beg of Him with most earnest prayer to perfect; that He Who hath now granted to count us in the number of His children may not at any time be grieved by our evil deeds. For we must always so serve Him with the good things He hath given us, that not only may He never, as an angry father, disinherit His children, but may never, as a dreadful LORD, incensed by our sins, deliver us to everlasting punishment, as most wicked servants who would not follow Him to glory.

Let us then at length arise, since the Scripture stirreth us up, saying: "It is time now for us to rise from sleep." And our eyes being opened to the deifying light, let us hear
with wondering ears what the Divine Voice admonisheth us, daily crying out: "Today if ye shall hear His voice, harden not your hearts." And again, "He that hath ears to hear, let him hear what the Spirit saith to the churches." And what saith He? "Come, my children, hearken to Me, I will teach you the fear of the LORD. Run while ye have the light of life, lest the darkness of death seize hold of you."

And the LORD, seeking His own workman in the multitude of the people to whom He thus crieth out, saith again: "Who is the man that will have life, and desireth to
see good days?" And if thou, hearing Him, answer, "I am he," God saith to thee: "If thou wilt have true and everlasting life, keep thy tongue from

evil and thy lips that they speak no guile. Turn from evil, and do good; seek peace and pursue it. And when you have done these things, My eyes will be upon you, and My ears will be open to your prayers; and before you call upon Me, I will say unto you, 'Behold, I am here.'" What can be sweeter to us, dearest brethren, than this voice of the LORD inviting us? Behold in his loving kindness the LORD shows to us the way of life.

Having our loins, therefore, girded with faith and the performance of good works, let us walk in His paths by the guidance of the gospel, that we may deserve to see Him who hath called us to His kingdom. And if we wish to dwell in the tabernacle of His kingdom, we shall by no means reach it unless we run thither by our good deeds. But let us ask the LORD with the prophet, saying to Him: "Lord, who shall dwell in Thy tabernacle, or who shall rest upon Thy holy hill?" After this question, brethren, let us hear the LORD answering, and showing to us the way to His tabernacle, and saying: "He that walketh without stain and worketh justice; he that speaketh truth in his heart, that hath not done guile with his tongue; he that hath done no evil to his neighbor, and hath not taken up a reproach against his neighbor;" he that hath brought the malignant evil one to naught, casting him out of his heart with all his suggestions, and hath taken his bad thoughts, while they were yet young, and dashed them down upon the (Rock) Christ. These are they, who fearing the LORD, are not puffed up with their own good works, but knowing that the good which is in them cometh not from themselves but from the LORD, magnify the LORD who worketh in them, saying with the prophet: "Not unto us, O LORD, not unto us, but unto Thy Name give the glory." So the Apostle Paul imputed nothing of His preaching to himself, but said: "By the grace of God I am what I am." And again he saith: "He that glorieth, let him glory in the LORD."

4 Jan.
5 May
4 Sept.

Hence also the LORD saith in the Gospel: "He that heareth these words of Mine, and doeth them, is like a wise man who built his house upon a rock: the floods came, the winds blew, and beat upon that house, and it fell not, because it was

5 Jan.
6 May
5 Sept.

founded upon a rock." And the LORD in fulfillment of these His words is waiting daily for us to respond by our deeds to His holy admonitions. Therefore are the days of our life lengthened for the amendment of our evil ways, as saith the Apostle, "Knowest thou not that the patience of God is leading thee to repentance?" For the merciful LORD saith: "I will not the death of a sinner, but that he should be converted and live."

Since then, brethren, we have asked of the LORD who is to inhabit His temple, we have heard His commands to those who are to dwell there: and if we fulfill those duties, 6 Jan.
7 May
6 Sept.
we shall be heirs of the kingdom of heaven. Our hearts, therefore, and our bodies must be made ready to fight under the holy obedience of His commands; and let us ask God to supply by the help of His grace what by nature is not possible to us. And if we would arrive at eternal life, escaping the pains of hell, then—while there is yet time, while we are still in the flesh, and are able to fulfill all these things by the light which is given us—we must hasten to do now what will profit us for all eternity.

We have, therefore, to establish a school of the LORD's service, in the setting forth of which we hope to order nothing that is harsh or rigorous. But if anything be 7 Jan.
8 May
7 Sept.
somewhat strictly laid down, according to the dictates of sound reason, for the amendment of vices or the preservation of charity, do not therefore fly in dismay from the way of salvation, whose beginning cannot but be strait and difficult. But as we go forward in our life and in faith, we shall with hearts enlarged and unspeakable sweetness of love run in the way of God's commandments; so that never departing from His guidance, but persevering in His teaching in the monastery until death, we may by patience share in the sufferings of Christ, that we may deserve to be partakers of His kingdom. Amen.

1

Of the Several Kinds of Monks and their way of Life

I T IS WELL KNOWN that there are four kinds of monks.
The *first* are the Cenobites: that is those in monasteries,
who live under a rule or an Abbot. The *second* are the
Anchorites or Hermits: that is those who, not in the first fervor of
religious life, but after long probation in the monastery, have learned by
the help and experience of many to fight against the devil; and going
forth well-armed from the ranks of their brethren to the single-handed
combat of the desert, are able, without the support of others, to fight by
the strength of their own arm, God helping them, against the vices of
the flesh and their evil thoughts. A *third* and most baneful kind of monks
are the Sarabites, who have been tried by no rule nor by the experience
of a master, as gold in the furnace; but, being as soft as lead, and still
serving the world in their works, are known by their tonsure to lie to
God. These in twos or threes, or even singly, without a shepherd, shut
up, not in the LORD's sheepfolds, but in their own, make a law to
themselves in the pleasure of their own desires: whatever they think fit
or choose to do, that they call holy; and what they like not, that they
consider unlawful.

The *fourth* kind of monks are those called "Girovagi," who spend all
their lives long wandering about divers provinces, staying in different
cells for three or four days at a time, ever roaming, with no stability,
given up to their own pleasures and to the snares of gluttony, and worse
in all things than the Sarabites. Of the most wretched life of these it is
better to say nothing than to speak. Leaving them alone therefore, let us

8 Jan.
9 May
8 Sept.

set to work, by the help of God, to lay down a rule for the Cenobites, that is, the strongest* kind of monks.

2

What Kind of Man the Abbot ought to be

A N ABBOT WHO IS worthy to rule over the monastery ought always to remember what he is called, and correspond to his name of superior by his deeds. For he is believed to hold the place of Christ in the monastery, since he is called by His name, as the Apostle saith: "Ye have received the spirit of the adoption of children, in which we cry Abba, Father." And therefore the Abbot ought not (God forbid) to teach, or ordain, or command anything contrary to the law of the LORD; but let his bidding and his doctrine be infused into the minds of his disciples like the leaven of divine justice.

9 Jan.
10 May
9 Sept.

Let the Abbot be ever mindful that at the dreadful judgment of God an account will have to be given both of his own teaching and of the obedience of his disciples. And let him know that to the fault of the shepherd shall be imputed any lack of profit which the father of the household may find in his sheep. Only then shall he be acquitted, if he shall have bestowed all pastoral diligence on his unquiet and disobedient flock, and employed all his care to amend their corrupt manner of life: then shall he be absolved in the

10 Jan.
11 May
10 Sept.

---

* *Fortissimum genus.* The special fortitude here attributed by St. Benedict to the cenobitical life consists in the perpetual and absolute submission to the will of another which that life entails. Some commentators see in the word *fortissimum* an allusion to the greater strength and security of community life as compared with the eremitical: inasmuch as where two or three are gathered together, there our LORD Himself, the tower of strength—*turris fortitudinis*—has specially promised to be in the midst of them.

judgment of the LORD, and may say to the LORD with the prophet: "I have not hidden Thy justice in my heart, I have declared Thy truth and Thy salvation, but they contemned and despised me." And then at length the punishment of death shall be inflicted on the disobedient sheep.

Therefore, when any one receiveth the name of Abbot, he ought to govern his disciples by a two-fold teaching: that is, he should show forth all goodness and holiness by his deeds rather than his words: declaring to the intelligent among his disciples the commandments of the LORD by words: but to the hard-hearted and the simple-minded setting forth the divine precepts by the example of his deeds. And let him show by his own actions that those things ought not to be done which he has taught his disciples to be against the law of God; lest, while preaching to others, he should himself become a castaway, and God should say to him in his sin: "Why dost thou declare My justice, and take My covenant in thy mouth? Thou hast hated discipline, and hast cast My words behind thee." And again, "Thou who sawest the mote in thy brother's eye, didst thou not see the beam in thine own?"

11 Jan.
12 May
11 Sept.

Let him make no distinction of persons in the monastery. Let not one be loved more than another, unless he be found to excel in good works or in obedience. Let not one of noble birth be put before him that was formerly a slave, unless some other reasonable cause exist for it. But if upon just consideration it should so seem good to the Abbot, let him arrange as he please concerning the place of any one whomsoever; but, otherwise, let them keep their own places; because, whether bond or free, we are all one in Christ, and bear an equal rank in the service of one LORD: "for with God there is no respecting of persons." Only for one reason are we preferred in His sight, if we be found to surpass others in good works and in humility. Let the Abbot, then, show equal love to all, and let the same discipline be imposed upon all according to their deserts.

12 Jan.
13 May
12 Sept.

For the Abbot in his doctrine ought always to observe the bidding of the Apostle, wherein he says: "Reprove,

13 Jan.
14 May
13 Sept.

17

entreat, rebuke:" mingling, as occasions may require, gentleness with severity; showing now the rigor of a master, now the loving affection of a father, so as sternly to rebuke the undisciplined and restless, and to exhort the obedient, mild, and patient to advance in virtue. And such as are negligent and haughty we charge him to reprove and correct. Let him not shut his eyes to the faults of offenders; but as soon as they appear, let him strive with all his might to root them out, remembering the fate of Heli, the priest of Silo. Those of good disposition and understanding let him, for the first or second time, correct only with words; but such as are froward and hard of heart, and proud, or disobedient, let him chastise with bodily stripes at the very first offense, knowing that it is written: "The fool is not corrected with words." And again: "Strike thy son with the rod, and thou shalt deliver his soul from death."

The Abbot ought always to remember what he is, and what he is called, and to know that to whom more is committed, from him more is required; and he must 14 Jan. 15 May 14 Sept. consider how difficult and arduous a task he hath undertaken, of ruling souls and adapting himself to many dispositions. Let him so accommodate and suit himself to the character and intelligence of each, winning some by kindness, others by reproof, others by persuasion, that he may not only suffer no loss in the flock committed to him, but may even rejoice in their virtuous increase.

Above all let him not, overlooking or undervaluing the salvation of the souls entrusted to him, be too solicitous for fleeting, earthly, and perishable things; but let him ever bear 15 Jan. 16 May 15 Sept. in mind that he hath undertaken the government of souls, of which he shall have to give an account. And that he may not complain for want of worldly substance, let him remember what is written: "Seek first the kingdom of God and His justice, and all these things shall be added unto you." And again: "Nothing is wanting to them that fear Him."

And let him know that he who hath undertaken the government of souls, must prepare himself to render an account of them. And whatever may be the number of the brethren under his care, let him be certainly assured that on the Day of Judgment he will have to give an account to the LORD of all these souls, as well as of his own. And thus, being ever fearful of the coming inquiry which the Shepherd will make into the state of the flock committed to him, while he is careful on other men's account, he will be solicitous also on his own. And. so, while correcting others by his admonitions, he will be himself cured of his own defects.

3

Of Calling the Brethren to Council

A S OFTEN AS ANY important matters have to be transacted in the monastery, let the Abbot call together the whole community, and himself declare what is the question to be settled. And, having heard the counsel of the brethren, let him consider within himself, and then do what he shall judge most expedient. We have said that all should be called to council, because it is often to the younger that the LORD revealeth what is best. But let the brethren give their advice with all subjection and humility, and not presume stubbornly to defend their own opinion; but rather let the matter rest with the Abbot's discretion, that all may submit to whatever he shall judge to be best. Yet, even as it becometh disciples to obey their master, so doth it behoove him to order all things prudently and with justice.

16 Jan.
17 May
16 Sept.

Let all, therefore, follow the Rule in all things as their guide, and let no man rashly turn aside from it. Let no one in the monastery follow the will of his own heart: nor let anyone presume insolently to contend with his Abbot, either within or without the monastery. But if he should so presume, let him be subjected to the discipline appointed by the Rule. The Abbot himself, however, must do everything with the fear of God and in observance of

17 Jan.
18 May
17 Sept.

the Rule: knowing that he will have without doubt to render to God, the most just Judge, an account of all his judgments. If it happen that less important matters have to be transacted for the good of the monastery, let him take counsel with the Seniors only, as it is written: "Do all things with counsel, and thou shalt not afterwards repent it."

4

What are the Instruments of Good Works

I N THE FIRST PLACE, to love the LORD God with all one's heart, all one's soul, and all one's strength. 18 Jan.
19 May
18 Sept.

  2. Then, one's neighbor as oneself.

  3. Then not to kill.

  4. Not to commit adultery.

  5. Not to steal.

  6. Not to covet.

  7. Not to bear false witness.

  8. To honor all men.

  9. Not to do to another what one would not have done to oneself.

  10. To deny oneself, in order to follow Christ.

  11. To chastise the body.

  12. Not to seek after delicate living.

  13. To love fasting.

  14. To relieve the poor.

  15. To clothe the naked.

  16. To visit the sick.

  17. To bury the dead.

  18. To help in affliction.

  19. To console the sorrowing.

  20. To keep aloof from worldly actions.

21. To prefer nothing to the love of Christ.

22. Not to give way to anger.

23. Not to harbor a desire of revenge.

19 Jan.
20 May
.19 Sept.

24. Not to foster guile in one's heart.

25. Not to make a feigned peace.

26. Not to forsake charity.

27. Not to swear, lest perchance one forswear oneself.

28. To utter truth from heart and mouth.

29. Not to render evil for evil.

30. To do no wrong to any one, yea, to bear patiently wrong done to oneself.

31. To love one's enemies.

32. Not to render cursing for cursing, but rather blessing.

33. To bear persecution for justice sake.

34. Not to be proud.

35. Not given to wine.

36. Not a glutton.

37. Not drowsy.

38. Not slothful.

39. Not a murmurer.

40. Not a detractor.

41. To put one's hope in God.

42. To attribute any good that one sees in oneself to God, and not to oneself.

43. But to recognize and always impute to oneself the evil that one doth.

44. To fear the Day of Judgment.

45. To be in dread of hell.

20 Jan.
21 May
20 Sept.

46. To desire with all spiritual longing everlasting life.

47. To keep death daily before one's eyes.

48. To keep guard at all times over the actions of one's life.

49. To know for certain that God sees one everywhere.

50. To dash down on the (Rock) Christ one's evil thoughts, the instant that they come into the heart:

51. And to lay them open to one's spiritual father.

52. To keep one's mouth from evil and wicked words.

53. Not to love much speaking.

54. Not to speak vain words or such as move to laughter.

55. Not to love much or excessive laughter.

56. To listen willingly to holy reading.

57. To apply oneself frequently to prayer.

58. Daily to confess one's past sins with tears and sighs to God, and to amend them for the time to come.

59. Not to fulfill the desires of the flesh: to hate one's own will.

60. To obey in all things the commands of the Abbot, even though he himself (which God forbid) should act otherwise: being mindful of that precept of the LORD: "What they say, do ye; but what they do, do ye not."

61. Not to wish to be called "holy" before one is so: but first *to be* holy, that one may be truly so called.

62. Daily to fulfill by one's deeds the commandments of God.

21 Jan.
22 May
21 Sept.

63. To love chastity.

64. To hate no man.

65. Not to give way to jealousy and envy.

66. Not to love strife.

67. To fly from vainglory.

68. To reverence the Seniors.

69. To love the juniors.

70. To pray for one's enemies in the love of Christ.

71. To make peace with an adversary before the setting of the sun.

72. And never to despair of the mercy of God.

Behold, these are the tools of the spiritual craft, which, if they be constantly employed day and night, and duly given back on the day of judgment, will gain for us from the LORD that reward which He Himself hath promised—"which eye hath not seen, nor ear heard; nor hath it entered into the heart of man to conceive what God hath prepared for them that love Him." And the workshop where we are to labor at all these things is the cloister of the monastery, and stability in the community.

5

Of Obedience

T HE FIRST DEGREE OF humility is obedience without delay. This becometh those who hold nothing dearer to them than Christ, and who on account of the holy servitude which they have taken upon them, either for fear of hell or for the glory of life everlasting, as soon as anything is ordered by the superior, suffer no more delay in doing it than if it had been commanded by God Himself. It is of these that the LORD saith: "At the hearing of the ear he hath obeyed Me." And, again, to teachers He saith: "He that heareth you heareth Me."

22 Jan.
23 May
22 Sept.

Such as these, therefore, leaving immediately their own occupations and forsaking their own will, with their hands disengaged, and leaving unfinished what they were about, with the speedy step of obedience follow by their deeds the voice of him who commands; and so as it were at the same instant the bidding of the master and the perfect fulfillment of the disciple are joined together in the swiftness of the fear of God by those who are moved with the desire of attaining eternal life. These, therefore, choose the narrow way, of which the LORD saith: "Narrow is the way which leadeth unto life;" so that living not by their own will, nor obeying their own desires and pleasures, but walking according to the judgment and command of another, and dwelling in community, they desire to have an Abbot over them. Such as these without doubt fulfill that saying of the LORD: "I came not to do Mine own will, but the will of Him who sent Me."

But this very obedience will then only be acceptable to 23 Jan.
God and sweet to men, if what is commanded be done not 24 May
fearfully, tardily, nor coldly, nor with murmuring, nor with
an answer, showing unwillingness; for the obedience which is given to superiors is given to God, since He Himself hath said: "He that heareth you, heareth Me." And it ought to be given by disciples with a good will, because "God loveth a cheerful giver." For if the disciple obey with ill-will, and murmur not only with his lips but even in his heart, although he fulfill the command, yet it will not be accepted by God, who regardeth the heart of the murmurer. And for such an action he shall gain no reward; nay, rather, he shall incur the punishment due to murmurers, unless he amend and make satisfaction.

6

Of the Practice of Silence

L ET US DO AS saith the prophet: "I said, I will take heed 24 Jan.
to my ways, that I sin not with my tongue, I have 25 May
placed a watch over my mouth; I became dumb and was
silent, and held my peace even from good things." Here the prophet showeth that if we ought at times to refrain even from good words for the sake of silence, how much more ought we to abstain from evil words, on account of the punishment due to sin. Therefore, on account of the importance of silence, let leave to speak be seldom granted even to perfect disciples,* although their conversation be good and holy and

---

* *Rara loquendi concedatur licentia.* "St. Benedict," observes Calmet, "as well as all the ancient Rules, preserves an unbroken silence on the subject of recreation." Nevertheless it appears certain, not only from this but from other passages in the Holy Rule, that

tending to edification; because it is written: "in much speaking thou shalt not avoid sin;" and elsewhere: "Death and life are in the power of the tongue." For it becometh the master to speak and to teach, but it beseemeth the disciple to be silent and to listen. And therefore, if anything has to be asked of the Superior, let it be done with all humility and subjection of reverence. But as for buffoonery or idle words, such as move to laughter, we utterly condemn them in every place, nor do we allow the disciple to open his mouth in such discourse.

7

Of Humility

T HE HOLY SCRIPTURE CRIETH out to us, brethren, saying, "Every one that exalteth himself shall be humbled, and he who humbleth himself shall be exalted." In saying this, it teacheth us that all exaltation is a kind of pride, against which the prophet showeth himself to be on his guard when he saith: "LORD, my heart is not exalted nor mine eyes lifted up; nor have I

25 Jan.
26 May
25 Sept.

---

conversation was not intended to be absolutely prohibited. Thus the brethren are directed (chap. 31) to ask at proper times for what they require; not to converse with one another except at proper times (chap. 48); and again (chap. 49) to talk less than usual during Lent. From very early times, fixed periods were appointed for conversation. The statutes of Adelard (*circ.* 822 A.D.) permit talking in the dormitory on certain occasions—the *Ordo Cluniacensis*, of the 11th century, lays down fixed rules and times for conversation in the cloister—and the early constitutions both of the Carthusian and Cistercian Orders explicitly legislate for conversations at regular times. (See Ven. Guigo, *Statute Carthus.*, c. 7, and *Monastic Cisterciens.*, p. 328, c. 5.) It is curious to note that it was anciently permitted to talk only on ferial days: silence and recollection were strictly prescribed on all festivals, *propter festivitatum reverentiam*; and this pious custom still prevails in some religious houses, *e.g.*, in certain convents of the Canonesses Regular of St. John Lateran.

walked in great things, nor in wonders above me." For why? "If I did not think humbly, but exalted my soul: like a child that is weaned from his mother, so wilt Thou requite my soul." Whence, brethren, if we wish to arrive at the highest point of humility, and speedily to reach that heavenly exaltation to which we can only ascend by the humility of this present life, we must by our ever-ascending actions erect such a ladder as that which Jacob beheld in his dream, by which the angels appeared to him descending and ascending. This descent and ascent signifieth nothing else than that we descend by self-exaltation and ascend by humility. And the ladder thus erected is our life in the world, which, if the heart be humbled, is lifted up by the LORD to heaven. The sides of the same ladder we understand to be our body and soul, in which our divine vocation hath placed various degrees of humility or discipline, which we must ascend.

The first degree of humility, then, is that a man always keeps the fear of God before his eyes, avoiding all forgetfulness; and that he be ever mindful of all that God hath commanded, bethinking himself that those who despise God will be consumed in hell for their sins, and that life everlasting is prepared for them that fear Him. And keeping himself at all times from sin and vice, whether of the thoughts, the tongue, the hands, the feet, or his own will, let him thus hasten to cut off the desires of the flesh.

26 Jan.
27 May
26 Sept.

Let him consider that he is always beheld from heaven by God, and that his actions are everywhere seen by the eye of the Divine Majesty, and are every hour reported to Him by His angels. This the prophet telleth us, when he showeth how God is ever present in our thoughts, saying: "God searcheth the heart and the reins." And again: "The LORD knoweth the thoughts of men." And he also saith: "Thou hast understood my thoughts afar off;" and "The thought of man shall confess to Thee." In order, therefore, that he may be on his guard against evil thoughts, let the humble brother say ever in his heart: "Then shall I be unspotted before Him, if I shall have kept me from mine iniquity."

27 Jan.
28 May
27 Sept.

We are, indeed, forbidden to do our own will by
Scripture, which saith to us: "Turn away from thine own will." And so too we beg of God in prayer that His will may be done in us. Rightly therefore are we taught not to do our own will, if we take heed to the warning of Scripture: "There are ways which to men seem right, but the ends thereof lead to the depths of hell:" or, again, when we tremble at what is said of the careless: "They are corrupt and have become abominable in their pleasures." And in regard to the desires of the flesh, we must believe that God is always present to us, as the prophet saith to the LORD: "O LORD, all my desire is before Thee."

Let us be on our guard then against evil desires, since
death hath its seat close to the entrance of delight; wherefore the Scripture commandeth us, saying: "Go not after thy concupiscences." Since, therefore, the eyes of the LORD behold the good and the evil; and the LORD is ever looking down from heaven upon the children of men, to see who hath understanding or is seeking God; and since the works of our hands are reported to Him day and night by the angels appointed to watch over us; we must be always on the watch, brethren, lest, as the prophet saith in the psalm, God should see us at any time declining to evil and become unprofitable; and lest, though He spare us now, because He is merciful and expecteth our conversion, He should say to us hereafter: "These things thou didst and I held My peace."

The second degree of humility is, that a man love not
his own will, nor delight in gratifying his own desires; but carry out in his deeds that saying of the LORD: "I came not to do mine own will, but the will of Him who sent me." And again Scripture saith: self-will hath punishment, but necessity wins a crown.*

---

* *Voluntas habet pœnam, et necessitas parit coronam*—*i.e.*, the necessity, self-imposed upon the monk, of living in subjection to the will of another, the reward of which will be a crown of glory hereafter. These words are not to be found in Holy Scripture, and it has been conjectured in consequence that by Scripture St. Benedict alludes to the writings of the Fathers, or early monastic saints. No such passage, however, is known to exist; and the reference is probably, as Paul the Deacon, Smaragdus and others have supposed, to the general sense of Scripture on the subject, rather than to any particular

The third degree of humility is, that a man for the love of God submit himself to his superior in all obedience; imitating the LORD, of whom the apostle saith: "He was made obedient even unto death." 31 Jan.
1 June
1 Oct.

The fourth degree of humility is, that if in this very obedience hard and contrary things, nay even injuries, are done to him, he should embrace them patiently with a quiet 1 Feb.
2 June
2 Oct. conscience, and not grow weary or give in, as the Scripture saith: "He that shall persevere to the end shall be saved." And again: "Let thy heart be comforted, and wait for the LORD." And showing how the faithful man ought to bear all things, however contrary, for the LORD, it saith in the person of the afflicted: "For Thee we suffer death all the day long; we are esteemed as sheep for the slaughter." And secure in their hope of the divine reward, they go on with joy, saying: "But in all these things we overcome, through Him who hath loved us." And so in another place Scripture saith: "Thou hast proved us, O God; Thou has tried us as silver is tried by fire; Thou hast led us into the snare, and hast laid tribulation on our backs." And in order to show that we ought to be under a superior, it goes on to say: "Thou hast placed men over our heads." Moreover, fulfilling the precept of the LORD by patience in adversities and injuries, they who are struck on one cheek offer the other: to him who taketh away their coat they leave also their cloak; and being forced to walk one mile, they go two. With Paul the apostle, they bear with false brethren, and bless those that curse them.

The fifth degree of humility is, not to hide from one's Abbot any of the evil thoughts that beset one's heart, or the 2 Feb.
3 June
3 Oct. sins committed in secret, but humbly to confess them. Concerning which the Scripture exhorteth us, saying: "Make known thy way unto the LORD, and hope in Him." And again: "Confess to the

---

passage. (*Cf.* Prov. 21:28; Eccles. 18:30; *ib.* 43:17; *ib.* 8:18; 2 Tim. 4:8; Jas. 1:12; 1 Pet. 5:4; Apoc. 2:10.)

In the Rule of St. Augustine, it is interesting to note, occur the words, *ubi scriptum est: Abominatio est Domino defigens omnium;* and this passage also is generally interpreted as being the general sense of Holy Scripture.

LORD, for He is good, and His mercy endureth forever." So also the prophet saith: "I have made known to Thee mine offence, and mine iniquities I have not hidden. I will confess against myself my iniquities to the LORD: and Thou hast forgiven the wickedness of my heart."

The sixth degree of humility is, for a monk to be contented with the meanest and worst of everything, and in all that is enjoined him to esteem himself a bad and worthless laborer, saying with the prophet: "I have been brought to nothing, and I knew it not: I am become as a beast before Thee, yet I am always with Thee." 3 Feb.
4 June
4 Oct.

The seventh degree of humility is, that he should not only call himself with his tongue lower and viler than all, but also believe himself in his inmost heart to be so, humbling himself, and saying with the prophet: "I am a worm and no man, the shame of men and the outcast of the people: I have been exalted, and cast down, and confounded." And again: "It is good for me that Thou hast humbled me, that I may learn Thy commandments." 4 Feb.
5 June
5 Oct.

The eighth degree of humility is, for a monk to do nothing except what is authorized by the common rule of the monastery, or the example of his seniors. 5 Feb.
6 June
6 Oct.

The ninth degree of humility is, that a monk refrain his tongue from speaking, keeping silent until a question he asked him, as the Scripture showeth: "In much talking thou shalt not avoid sin:" and, "The talkative man shall not be directed upon the earth." 6 Feb.
7 June
7 Oct.

The tenth degree of humility is, that he be not easily moved and prompt to laughter, because it is written: "The fool lifteth up his voice in laughter." 7 Feb.
8 June
8 Oct.

The eleventh degree of humility is, that when a monk speaketh, he do so gently and without laughter, humbly, gravely, with few and reasonable words, and that he be not noisy in his speech, as it is written: "A wise man is known by the fewness of his words." 8 Feb.
9 June
9 Oct.

The twelfth degree of humility is, that the monk, not 9 Feb. only in his heart but also in his very exterior, always show 10 June 10 Oct. his humility to all who see him: that is, in the work of God, in the oratory, in the monastery, in the garden, on the road, in the field, or wherever he may be, whether sitting, walking or standing, with head always bent down, and eyes fixed on the earth, that he ever think of the guilt of his sins, and imagine himself already present before the terrible judgment-seat of God: always saying in his heart what the publican in the Gospel said with his eyes fixed on the earth: "LORD, I a sinner am not worthy to raise mine eyes to heaven." And again, with the prophet: "I am bowed down and humbled on every side."

Having, therefore, ascended all these degrees of humility, the monk will presently arrive at that love of God which, being perfect, casteth out fear: whereby he shall begin to keep, without labor, and as it were naturally and by custom, all those precepts which he had hitherto observed through fear: no longer through dread of hell, but for the love of Christ, and of a good habit and a delight in virtue: which God will vouchsafe to manifest by the Holy Spirit in his laborer, now cleansed from vice and sin.

8

Of the Divine Office at Night

IN WINTER TIME, THAT is, from the first of November 10 Feb. until Easter, the brethren shall rise at what may be 11 June 11 Oct. reasonably calculated to be the eighth hour of the night;* so that having rested till some time past midnight, they may rise having had

---

* *Octava hora.* The Romans divided the night as well as the day into twelve equal divisions or hours; but as the night commenced at sunset and continued till sunrise, the length of these hours would vary according to the season, being longer in winter and

their full sleep. And let the time that remains after the Night-Office be spent in study by those brethren who have still some part of the psalter and lessons to learn. But from Easter to the first of November let the hour for the Night-Office be so arranged that, after a very short interval, during which the brethren may go out for the necessities of nature, Lauds, which are to be said at day-break, may follow without delay.

9

How many Psalms are to be Said at the Night-Hours

I N WINTER TIME, AFTER beginning with the verse, "O God, come to my assistance; O Lord, make haste to help me," with the *Gloria,* let the words, "O Lord, Thou wilt open my lips, and my mouth shall declare Thy praise," be next repeated thrice; then the third Psalm, with a *Gloria,* after which the ninety-fourth Psalm is to be said or sung, with an antiphon. Next let a hymn follow, and then six Psalms with antiphons. These being said, and also a

11 Feb.
12 June
12 Oct.

shorter in summer. Calculated in this way, the eighth hour of the night would of course vary with the time of year, as well as with the latitude of the various countries. At mid-winter, in the latitude of Rome, the eighth hour would commence about 3 A.M., and end about 4. St. Benedict seems to lay down in this chapter that the hour for the night-office is to vary according to the above mode of reckoning. (See Perez, *Comment.,* c. viii. 13.) Paul the Deacon, however, with Turrecremata and others, interprets the words *juxta considerationem rationis* to mean that the eighth hour was always to be calculated from the same time, either from the first of November or the vernal equinox.

The *meditatio,* in which the Rule prescribes that the time remaining after the night-office is to be spent, means, as is evident from the context, study, and not meditation in the modern sense of the word. St. Benedict does not lay down any fixed time for mental prayer, apart from the Divine Office. We know, however, that it was the regular practice in his monasteries, from his life by St. Gregory (Dialogues, Bk. ii. c. 4), which speaks of "the hour when the singing of psalms was ended, and the monks betook themselves to prayer."

versicle, let the Abbot give the blessing: and, all being seated, let three lessons be read by the brethren in turns, from the book on the lectern. Between the lessons let three responsories be sung—two of them without a *Gloria,* but after the third let the reader say the *Gloria:* and as soon as he begins it, let all rise from their seats out of honor and reverence to the Holy Trinity. Let the divinely inspired books, both of the Old and New Testaments, be read at the Night-Office, and also the commentaries upon them written by the most renowned, orthodox and Catholic Fathers. After these three lessons with their responsories, let six more Psalms follow, to be sung with an *Alleluia.* Then let a lesson from the Apostle be said by heart, with a verse and the petition of the Litany, that is, *Kyrie eleison.* And so let the Night-Office come to an end.

10

How the Night-Office is to be Said in Summertime

FROM EASTER TO THE first of November let the same number of Psalms be recited as prescribed above; only that no lessons are to be read from the book, on account of the shortness of the night: but instead of those three lessons let one from the Old Testament be said by heart, followed by a short responsory, and the rest as before laid down; so that never less than twelve Psalms, not counting the third and ninety-fourth, be said at the Night-Office.

12 Feb.
13 June
13 Oct.

11

How the Night-Office is to be Said on Sundays

ON SUNDAY LET THE brethren rise earlier for the Night-Office, which is to be arranged as follows. When six Psalms and a versicle have been sung (as already prescribed), all being seated in order in their stalls, let four lessons with their responsories be read from the book, as before: and to the last responsory only let the reader add a *Gloria*, all reverently rising as soon as he begins it. After the lessons let six more Psalms follow in order, with their antiphons and versicle as before; and then let four more lessons, with their responsories, be read in the same way as the former. Next let three canticles from the Prophets be said, as the Abbot shall appoint, which canticles are to be sung with an *Alleluia*. After the versicle, and the blessing given by the Abbot, let four more lessons from the New Testament be read as before; and at the end of the fourth responsory, let the Abbot begin the hymn, *Te Deum laudamus*. After the hymn, let the Abbot read the lesson from the Gospel, while all stand in awe and reverence. The Gospel being ended, let all answer *Amen*. Then let the Abbot go on with the hymn, *Te decet laus;* and after the blessing hath been given,* let them begin Lauds. This order for the Night-Office is always to be observed on Sunday, alike in summer and in winter, unless perchance (which God forbid) they rise too late, in which case the lessons or responsories must be somewhat shortened.† Let all care,

---

* *Data benedictione.* The *benedictio* here referred to is the collect, or prayer of the day, said after the Gospel. The word *benedictio* is often used with the signification of prayer: *e.g.*, in chapters 35 and 38, where the weekly reader and servers are directed to receive the blessing before entering on their offices. So, conversely, in chapter 49, the word *oratio* is used in the sense of the blessing given by the Abbot: "Quod unusquisque offert, cum ejus fiat *oratione* et voluntate."

† *Aliquid de lectionibus breviandum.* Anciently the length of the lessons was not fixed as at present, but the signal for their conclusion was given by the Superior, who, when he

however, be taken that this do not happen; but if it should, let him, through whose neglect it hath come to pass, make satisfaction for it in the oratory.

12

How the Solemn Office of Lauds is to be Said

A T LAUDS ON SUNDAY let the sixty-sixth Psalm first be said straight on* without an antiphon. After this let the fiftieth Psalm be said, with an *Alleluia,* and then the hundred and seventeenth and the sixty-second. Then the *Benedicite* and Psalms of praise,† a lesson from the Apocalypse, said by heart, a responsory, a hymn, a versicle, a canticle out of the Gospel, and the Litany, and so end.

14 Feb.
15 June
15 Oct.

---

thought fit, pronounced the words *Tu autem Domine,* the reader concluding *miserere nobis.* Charlemagne, we are told, when presiding at the office in his private chapel, coughed *(signum ex gutture faciebat)* as a signal for the reader to cease. In some monasteries it was the custom for the cantor to mark previously with a drop of wax, or with his finger-nail, the point where the lessons were to conclude. The present discipline of the Church, which has not only fixed the length of the lessons, but binds every professed monk to the recitation of the Office in its integrity, has of course superseded the injunction here given by St. Benedict.

* *In directum.* Bernard of M. Cassino and Calmet suppose this to mean simple recitation without chant. The more probable interpretation is that the verses are to be said consecutively, unlike, *e.g.,* the psalm *Venite* at matins, which is interspersed with antiphons. Dom Leclerg, in an article in the "Dictionnaire d' Archéologie Chrétienne" (fasc. viii., col. 2299) gives reasons for his opinion that a psalm recited *in directum* was said by the whole choir together, not by alternate sides; and this view is corroborated by a rubric in the Ambrosian Breviary: "Psalmus directus in Dominicis diebus qui ab utroque choro stante dicitur communiter, et non alternatim." (See note "†" on page 38.)

† Psalm 148, 149, 150.

13

How Lauds are to be said on Week-days

O N WEEK-DAYS LET LAUDS be celebrated in the following manner. Let the sixty-sixth Psalm be said without an antiphon, as on Sundays, and somewhat slowly,
in order that all may be in time for the fiftieth, which is to be said with an antiphon. After this let two other Psalms be said according to custom; that is, on Monday, the fifth and thirty-fifth: on Tuesday, the forty-second and fifty-sixth: on Wednesday, the sixty-third and sixty-fourth: on Thursday, the eighty-seventh and eighty-ninth: on Friday, the seventy-fifth and ninety-first: and on Saturday, the hundred and forty-second and the Canticle from Deuteronomy, which must be divided into two *Gloria's.* But on the other days let canticles from the prophets be said, each on its proper day, according to the practice of the Roman Church. Then let the psalms of praise follow, and after them a lesson from the Apostle, to be said by heart, a responsory, a hymn, a versicle, a canticle out of the Gospel, the Litany, and so conclude.

The office of Lauds and Vespers, however, must never conclude without the Lord's Prayer being said aloud by the Superior, so that all may hear it, on account of the thorns of
scandal* which are wont to arise; so that the brethren, by the covenant which they make in that prayer when they say, "Forgive us as we

---

* *Scandalorum spinas.* In order to remind the brethren of the duty of mutual concord and charity, and the scandalous consequences of the opposite vices, St. Benedict here orders an exception to the general practice of saying the Lord's Prayer in secret, which was part of the *disciplina arcani* of the early Church. The Prayer was considered too sacred to be used or even heard by those not fully initiated into the Faith; and hence the catechumens, who left the Church at the offertory of the Mass, would not be present at the solemn chanting of the *Pater noster.* In the Roman Office the Lord's Prayer is still said in secret wherever it occurs, with very few exceptions.

forgive," may cleanse themselves of such faults. But at the other Offices let the last part only of the prayer be said aloud, so that all may answer: "But deliver us from evil."

14

How the Night-Office is to be Said on Saints' Days

O N THE FESTIVALS of Saints, and all other solemnites, let the Office be ordered as we have prescribed for Sundays: except that the Psalms, antiphons, and lessons suitable to the day are to be said. Their number, however, shall remain as we have appointed above.

17 Feb.
18 June
18 Oct.

15

At what times of the year "Alleluia" is to be said

F ROM THE HOLY FEAST of Easter until Pentecost, without interruption, let *Alleluia* be said both with the Psalms and the responsories. From Pentecost until the beginning of Lent, it is to be said at the Night-Office with the six latter Psalms only. But on every Sunday out of Lent let the Canticles*—Lauds, Prime, Tierce, Sext and None—be said with *Alleluia*. Vespers, however,

18 Feb.
19 June
19 Oct.

The *Litanice* spoken of in this chapter are the *Kyrie eleison, Christe eleison,* and such, immediately preceding the *Pater noster* and Collect, with which the Office concludes.

* In the third nocturn of the Night-Office.

with an antiphon. The responses are never to be said with *Alleluia*,
except from Easter to Pentecost.

16

How the Work of God is to be done in the Day-time

A S THE PROPHET SAITH: "Seven times in the day have
I given praise to Thee." And we shall observe this
sacred number of seven if, at the times of Lauds, Prime,
Tierce, Sext, None, Vespers and Compline, we fulfill the duties of our
service. For it was of these hours of the day that he said: "Seven times in
the day have I given praise to Thee:" just as the same prophet saith of
the night watches: "At midnight I arose to give Thee praise." At these
times, therefore, let us sing the praises of our Creator for the judgments
of His justice: that is, at Lauds, Prime, Tierce, Sext, None, Vespers and
Compline; and at night let us arise to praise Him.

19 Feb.
20 June
20 Oct.

17

How many Psalms are to be Sung at these Hours

W E HAVE NOW DISPOSED the order of the psalmody
for the Night-Office and for Lauds: let us proceed
to arrange for the remaining Hours. At Prime, let three
Psalms be said, separately and not under one *Gloria*. The hymn at this
Hour is to follow the verse, *Deus in adjutorium*, before the Psalms be
begun. Then, at the end of the three Psalms, let one lesson be said, with

20 Feb.
21 June
21 Oct.

a versicle, the *Kyrie eleison,* and the Collect.* Tierce, Sext, and None are to be recited in the same way, that is, the Verse, the hymn proper to each hour, three Psalms, the lesson and versicle, *Kyrie eleison,* with the Collect. If the community be large, let the Psalms be sung with antiphons; but if small, let them be sung straight forward.† Let the Vesper Office consist of four Psalms with antiphons: after the Psalms a lesson is to be recited; then a responsory, a hymn and versicle, the canticle from the Gospel, the Litany and Lord's Prayer, and finally the Collect. Let Compline consist of the recitation of three Psalms, to be said straight on without antiphons; then the hymn for that Hour, one lesson, the versicle, *Kyrie eleison,* the blessing and the Collect.

---

* *Missæ sint.* The word *missa* is used by ecclesiastical writers in various significations: (1) The sacrifice of the Mass; (2) the lessons sung at the Night-Office; (3) a canonical hour itself (*cf.* Cassian, lib. II., c. 13—"Post *missam nocturnam* dormire non oportet"); (4) a collect or prayer said at the end of the Office (Concil. Milevitanum, can. 12. "Orationes seu *missæ quæ* prohibitæ fuerint in Concilio") (5) instead of *missio,* as at the end of Mass: "Ite, *missa est*"—"Go, you are dismissed." (So St. Cyprian uses *remissa* for *remissio.*) The word can only be used here in one of the two latter senses; and though both interpretations have found advocates, the former, namely, that referring it to the final prayer or collect, is supported by the principal commentators, as Bernard of M. Cassino, Turrecremata, Caramuel, Boherius, Martene, and others. It is certain, from the Holy Rule itself, that a prayer was prescribed at the end of the Office (see chapter 47); and it would therefore be natural to find it ordered here, where directions for the Divine Office are being minutely laid down by St. Benedict.

† *Si vero minor, in directum psallantur.* Calmet well points out here that what is prescribed, in the case of a small community, cannot be the mere omission of the antiphon before and after the Psalms, which would make no appreciable difference in the length of the Office. The learned F. Tomasi (*In Responsoria et Antiphonaria Eccl. Roman.,* 1686) has shown that it was anciently the custom to interpolate an antiphon, often after every verse of the psalm, as is still the case at the *Venite* of matins, and as we find in Psalm 135, where the words "For His mercy endureth forever" are added as an antiphon to each verse. It was no doubt this frequent repetition of the antiphon which St. Benedict allowed to be omitted.

Congregatio minor is usually interpreted to mean one consisting of less than twelve members, which was the primitive number of a Benedictine Community. St. Gregory (*Dialogues,* B. ii., c. 3) tells us that St. Benedict "built [at Subiaco] twelve Abbeys, and in each of them he placed twelve monks."

18

In what Order the Psalms are to be Said

FIRST OF ALL LET this verse be said: "O God, come to my assistance; O Lord, make haste to help me," and the *Gloria,* followed by the Hymn proper to each Hour. At 21 Feb.
22 June
22 Oct. Prime on Sunday four parts of the hundred and eighteenth Psalm are to be said. At the other Hours, that is, Tierce, Sext, and None, let three parts of the same Psalm be said. At Prime on Monday let three Psalms be said, namely the first, second, and sixth; and so in the same way every day until Sunday let three Psalms be said at Prime in order, up to the nineteenth; the ninth and the seventeenth, however, being divided into two *Gloria's.* It will thus come about that at the Night-Office on Sunday we shall always begin with the twentieth Psalm.

At Tierce, Sext and None on Monday are to be said the nine remaining parts of the hundred and eighteenth Psalm, 22 Feb.
23 June
23 Oct. three parts at each Hour. This Psalm having thus been said through in two days, that is Sunday and Monday, let the nine Psalms from the hundred and nineteenth to the hundred and twenty-second be said on Tuesday at Tierce, Sext, and None—three at each Hour. And these Psalms are to repeated at the same Hours every day until Sunday; the arrangement, moreover, of hymns, lessons and versicles remaining the same throughout, so as always to begin on Sunday from the hundred and eighteenth Psalm.

Vespers are to be sung every day with four Psalms. And let these begin from the hundred and ninth, and go on 23 Feb.
24 June
24 Oct. to the hundred and forty-seventh, omitting those of their number which are set apart for other Hours—that is, from the hundred and seventeenth to the hundred and twenty-seventh, the hundred and thirty-third, and the hundred and forty-second. All the rest are to be said at Vespers. And as there are three Psalms wanting, let those of the

aforesaid number which are somewhat long be divided, namely the hundred and thirty-eighth, the hundred and forty-third, and the hundred and forty-fourth. But let the hundred and sixteenth, as it is short, be joined to the hundred and fifteenth.

The order of the Psalms at Vespers being thus disposed, let the rest, that is the lessons, responses, hymns, verses, and canticles, be said as already laid down. At Compline the same Psalms are to be repeated every day: namely the fourth, ninetieth, and hundred and thirty-third.

The order of psalmody for the Day-Hours being now arranged let all the remaining Psalms be equally distributed among the seven Night-Offices, dividing the longer Psalms among them, and assigning twelve to each night. Above all, we recommend that if this arrangement of the Psalms be displeasing to any one, he should, if he think fit, order it otherwise; taking care in any case that the whole Psalter of a hundred and fifty Psalms be recited every week, and always begun afresh at the Night-Office on Sunday. For those monks would show themselves very slothful in the divine service who said in the course of a week less than the entire Psalter, with the usual canticles; since we read that our holy fathers resolutely performed in a single day what I pray we tepid monks may achieve in a whole week.

24 Feb.
25 June
25 Oct.

19

Of the Discipline of Saying the Divine Office

WE BELIEVE THAT THE Divine presence is everywhere, and that the eyes of the LORD behold the good and the evil in every place. Especially should we believe this, without any doubt, when we are assisting at the Work of God. Let us, then, ever remember what the prophet saith: "Serve the LORD in fear;" and again, "Sing ye wisely;" and, "In the sight of the

24 Feb.
26 June
26 Oct.

angels I will sing praises unto Thee." Therefore let us consider how we ought to behave ourselves in the presence of God and of His angels, and so assist at the Divine Office, that our mind and our voice may accord together.

20

Of Reverence at Prayer

I F, WHEN WE WISH to make any request to men in power, we presume not to do so except with humility and reverence; how much more ought we with all lowliness and purity of devotion to offer our supplications to the LORD God of all things? And let us remember that not for our much speaking, but for our purity of heart and tears of compunction shall we be heard. Our prayer, therefore, ought to be short and pure, except it be perchance prolonged by the inspiration of Divine Grace. But let prayer made in common always be short: and at the signal given by the Superior, let all rise together.

25 Feb.
27 June
27 Oct.

21

Of the Deans of the Monastery

S HOULD THE COMMUNITY be large, let there be chosen from it certain brethren of good repute and holy life, and appointed Deans. Let them carefully direct their deaneries in all things according to the commandments of God and the

26 Feb.
28 June
28 Oct.

will of their Abbot. And let such men be chosen Deans as the Abbot may safely trust to share his burdens: let them not be chosen according to order, but for the merit of their lives and for their wisdom and learning. And should any one of them, being puffed up with pride, be found worthy of blame, and after being thrice corrected, refuse to amend, let him be deposed, and one who is worthy put in his place. And we order the same to be done with regard to the Prior.

22

How the Monks are to Sleep

LET THEM SLEEP EACH in a separate bed, receiving bedding suitable to their manner of life, as the Abbot shall appoint. If possible, let all sleep in one place:* but if the number do not permit of this, let them repose by tens or twenties with the seniors who have charge of them. Let a candle burn constantly in the cell until morning. Let them sleep clothed, and girded with belts or cords—but not with knives at their sides, lest perchance they wound themselves in their sleep—and thus be always ready, so that when the signal is given they may rise without delay, and hasten each to forestall the other in going to the Work of God, yet with all gravity and modesty. Let not the younger brethren have their beds by themselves, but among those of the seniors. And when they rise for the Work of God, let them gently encourage one another, because of the excuses of the drowsy.

27 Feb.
29 June
29 Oct.

---

* *In uno loco dormiant.* This rule was strictly observed for many centuries. Separate cells are expressly forbidden in all the ancient Rules; and in A.D. 1341 we find the General Chapter of the English Benedictines, and a hundred years later that of Cluny, repeating the same prohibition. The dormitory was only entered at night, and everything in the way of reading and study in the early monasteries was carried on in the cloister, from which seculars were for centuries strictly excluded.

23

Of Excommunication for Offenses

I F ANY BROTHER SHALL be found contumacious, or 28 Feb. disobedient, or proud, or a murmurer, or in any way 30 June transgressing the Holy Rule, and contemning the orders of 30 Oct. his seniors; let him, according to our LORD's commandment, be once or twice privately admonished by his elders. If he do not amend, let him be rebuked in public before all. But if even then he do not correct himself, let him be subjected to excommunication, provided that he understand the nature of the punishment. Should he, however, prove incorrigible, let him undergo corporal chastisement.

24

What the Measure of Excommunication should be

T HE MEASURE OF excommunication or chastisement 1 Mar. should be meted out according to the gravity of the 1 July offence, the estimation of which shall be left to the 31 Oct. judgment of the Abbot. If any brother be found guilty of lighter faults, let him be excluded from the common table. And this shall be the rule for one so deprived: he shall intone neither Psalm nor antiphon in the Oratory, nor shall he read a lesson, until he have made satisfaction. Let him take his meals alone, after those of the brethren; so that if, for example, the brethren eat at the sixth hour, let him eat at the ninth: if they eat at the ninth, let him eat in the evening, until by proper satisfaction he obtain pardon.

25

Of Graver Faults

2 Mar.
2 July
1 Nov.

L ET THAT BROTHER WHO is found guilty of a more grievous offense be excluded both from the table and from the Oratory, and let none of the brethren consort with him or speak to him. Let him be alone at the work enjoined him, and continue in penance and sorrow, remembering that dreadful sentence of the Apostle, "That such a one is delivered over to Satan for the destruction of the flesh, that his spirit may be saved in the day of the LORD." Let him take his portion of food alone, in the measure and at the time that the Abbot shall think best for him. Let none of those who pass by bless him, nor the food that is given him.

26

Of those who, without Leave of the Abbot, Consort with the Excommunicate

3 Mar.
3 July
2 Nov.

I F ANY BROTHER presume without the Abbot's leave to hold any intercourse whatever with an excommunicated brother, or to speak with him, or to send him a message, let him incur the same punishment of excommunication.

27

How Careful the Abbot should be of the Excommunicate

L ET THE ABBOT SHOW all care and solicitude towards the offending brethren, for "they that are whole need not a physician, but they that are sick." To which end he ought, as a wise physician, to use every means in his power, sending some brethren of mature years and wisdom,* who may, as it were secretly, console the wavering brother, and induce him to make humble satisfaction. Let them comfort him, that he be not overwhelmed by excess of sorrow; but as the Apostle saith, "Let charity be strengthened towards him," and let all pray for him. For the Abbot is bound to use the greatest care, and to strive with all possible prudence and zeal, not to lose any one of the sheep committed to him. He must know that he hath undertaken the charge of weakly souls, and not a tyranny over the strong; and let him fear the threat of the prophet, through whom God saith: "What ye saw to be fat that ye took to yourselves, and what was diseased ye cast away." Let him imitate the loving example of the Good Shepherd, who, leaving the ninety and nine sheep on the mountains, went to seek one which had gone astray, on whose weakness He had such compassion that He offered to lay it on His own sacred shoulders and so bring it back to the flock.

---

* *Sympæctas:* from the Greek συμ-παίξειν, literally play fellows, *collusores*, and hence those who combine together for any purpose—not necessarily an unlawful one, as is now implied by "collusion." The *sympæctæ* here referred to may perhaps signify those brethren who had been brought up in the Monastery from childhood with the delinquent, and might thus be supposed to have special influence with him; or, more probably, the allusion is to the combination, or conspiracy, so to speak, between the Abbot and some of the elder and more discreet members of his community, with the object of bringing the refractory brother to a better mind.

28

Of those Who, being Often Corrected, do not Amend

I F ANY BROTHER WHO has been frequently corrected for
some fault, or even excommunicated, does not amend 5 Mar.
5 July
4 Nov.
let a more severe chastisement be applied: that is, let the
punishment of stripes be administered to him. But if even then he does
not correct himself, or perchance (which God forbid), pulled up with
pride, even wish to defend his deeds: then let the Abbot act like a wise
physician. If he hath applied fomentations and the unction of his
admonitions, the medicine of the Holy Scriptures, and the last remedy of
excommunication or corporal chastisement, and if he see that his labors
are of no avail, let him add what is still more powerful his own prayers
and those of all the brethren for him, that God, who is all-powerful, may
work the cure of the sick brother. But if he be not healed even by this
means, then at length let the Abbot use the sword of separation, as the
Apostle saith: "Put away the evil one from you." And again: "If the
faithless one depart, let him depart," lest one diseased sheep should taint
the whole flock.

29

Whether the Brethren who Leave the Monastery
are to be Received Again

I F ANY BROTHER, WHO through his own fault departeth
or is cast out of the Monastery, be willing to return, let 6 Mar.
6 July
5 Nov.

him first undertake to amend entirely the fault for which he went away; and then let him be received back into the lowest place, that thus his humility may be tried. Should he again depart, let him be taken back until the third time: knowing that after this all return will be denied to him.

30

How the Younger Boys are to be Corrected

E VERY AGE AND understanding should have its proper measure of discipline. As often, therefore, as boys, or others under age, or unable to understand the greatness of the penalty of excommunication, commit faults, let them be punished by severe fasting or sharp stripes, in order that they may be cured.

7 Mar.
7 July
6 Nov.

31

What Kind of Man the Cellarer of the Monastery is to be

L ET THERE BE CHOSEN out of the community, as Cellarer of the Monastery, a man wise and of mature character, temperate, not a great eater, not haughty, nor headstrong, nor arrogant, not slothful, nor wasteful, but a God-fearing man, who may be like a father to the whole community. Let him have the care of everything, but do nothing without leave of the Abbot. Let him take heed to what is commanded him, and not sadden his brethren. If a brother ask him for anything unreasonably, let him not treat him

8 Mar.
8 July
7 Nov.

with contempt and so grieve him, but reasonably and with all humility refuse what he asks for amiss. Let him be watchful over his own soul, remembering always that saying of the Apostle, that "he that hath ministered well, purchaseth to himself a good degree." Let him have especial care of the sick, of the children, of guests and of the poor, knowing without doubt that he will have to render an account of all these on the Day of Judgment. Let him look upon all the vessels and goods of the Monastery as though they were the consecrated vessels of the altar. Let him not think that he may neglect anything: let him not be given to covetousness, nor wasteful, nor a squanderer of the goods of the Monastery; but do all things in proper measure, and according to the bidding of his Abbot.

Let him above all things have humility; and to him on whom he hath nothing else to bestow, let him give at least a kind answer, as it is written: "A good word is above the best gift." Let him have under his care all that the Abbot may enjoin him, and presume not to meddle with what is forbidden him. Let him distribute to the brethren their appointed allowance of food, without arrogance* or delay, that they be not scandalized: mindful of what the Word of God declareth him to deserve, who "shall scandalize one of these little ones:" namely, "that a mill-stone be hanged about his neck and that he be drowned in the depths of the sea." If the community be large, let helpers be given to him, by whose aid he may with peace of mind discharge the office committed to him. Let such things as are necessary be given and asked for at befitting times, that no one may be troubled nor grieved in the house of God.

9 Mar.
9 July
8 Nov.

---

* *Sine* typo. So all the manuscripts, but the word is nevertheless clearly not from τύπος (a figure or image) but from τύφος—pride (literally, the *smoke* obscuring the soul). The word *typhus* in this sense is not uncommon in late Latin. *Cf.* Arnobius II. 43, &c. So St. Augustine (*Epist.* xxii. 29), speaking of the oblations at funerals, says that they should be offered "sine *typho* et cum alacritate." And St. Gregory speaks of *typhus superbiæ:* (*Epist.* 1. vi. 8). Both these passages have *typhus* in some MSS., owing, possibly, to the transcriber's ignorance of Greek, and to the consequently unfamiliar look of the word in its Latin form.

32

Of the Iron Tools, and Property of the Monastery

L ET THE ABBOT APPOINT brethren, on whose manner
of life and character he can rely, to the charge of the
iron tools, clothes, and other property of the Monastery;
and let him consign to their care, as he shall think fit, the things to be
kept and collected after use. Of these let the Abbot keep a list, so that as
the brethren in turn succeed to different employments, he may know
what he giveth and receiveth back. If anyone treat the property of the
Monastery in a slovenly or negligent manner, let him be corrected; and if
he do not amend, let him be subjected to the discipline of the Rule.

10 Mar.
10 July
9 Nov.

33

Whether Monks ought to have anything of their Own

T HE VICE OF PRIVATE ownership is above all to be cut
off from the Monastery by the roots. Let none
presume to give or receive anything without leave of the
Abbot, nor to keep anything as their own, either book or writing-tablet
or pen, or anything whatsoever; since they are permitted to have neither
body nor will in their own power. But all that is necessary they may
hope to receive from the father of the Monastery: nor are they allowed
to keep anything which the Abbot has not given, or at least permitted
them to have. Let all things be common to all, as it is written: "Neither
did anyone say that aught which he possessed was his own." But if any

11 Mar.
11 July
10 Nov.

one shall be found to indulge in this most baneful vice, and after one or two admonitions do not amend, let him be subjected to correction.

34

Whether all ought alike to Receive what is Needful

A S IT IS WRITTEN: "Distribution was made to every man, according as he had need." Herein we do not say that there should be respecting of persons—God forbid—but consideration for infirmities. Let him, therefore, that hath need of less give thanks to God, and not be grieved; and let him who requireth more be humbled for his infirmity, and not made proud by the kindness shown to him: and so all the members of the family shall be at peace. Above all, let not the evil of murmuring show itself by the slightest word or sign on any account whatsoever. If anyone be found guilty herein, let him be subjected to very severe punishment.

12 Mar.
12 July
11 Nov.

35

Of the Weekly Servers in the Kitchen

L ET THE BRETHREN WAIT on one another in turn, so that none be excused from the work of the kitchen, except he be prevented by sickness or by some more necessary employment: for thus is gained a greater reward and an increase of charity. But let assistance be given to the weak, that they may not do their work with sadness: and let all have help according to the

13 Mar.
13 July
12 Nov.

number of the community and the situation of the place. If the community be large, let the Cellarer be excused from work in the kitchen, and also those, as already mentioned, who are occupied in more urgent business. Let the rest serve each other in turn with all charity. Let him who endeth his week in the kitchen, make all things clean on Saturday, and wash the towels wherewith the brethren dry their hands and feet. Let both him who goeth out and him who is coming in wash the feet of all. Let him hand over to the Cellarer the vessels of his office, clean and whole; and let the Cellarer deliver the same to him who entereth, that he may know what he giveth and what he receiveth.

Let the weekly servers take each a cup of drink and a piece of bread over and above the appointed portion, one hour before the time for reflection, that so they may serve

14 Mar.
14 July
13 Nov.

their brethren, when the hour cometh, without murmuring or great labor. On solemn days, however, let them forbear until after Mass.* On Sunday, as soon as Lauds are ended, let both the incoming and the outgoing servers fall on their knees before all, in the Oratory, and ask their prayers. Let him who endeth his week, say this verse: "Blessed art Thou, LORD God, who hast helped me and comforted me;" which being thrice repeated, he shall receive the blessing.† Let him that beginneth his week follow, and say: "O God, come to my assistance: O LORD, make haste to help me." Let this likewise be thrice repeated by all; and having received the blessing, let him enter on his office.

---

* *Usque ad missas sustineant.* That is, until after Holy Communion, which the servers would approach, with the rest of the Community, on all Sundays and holidays, at the one mass which was then celebrated in the Monastery. We see by this passage that St. Benedict inculcated the duty of communicating on all festivals of the Church, in emulation of the Egyptian and Syrian monks, who, as Cassian tells us (III. 2), observed the same pious practice. We learn from the early Rules that the monks were accustomed to communicate standing; and this was continued by the Congregation of Cluny, among others, down to later times.

† *Accipiat benedictionem.* See note on page 33.

36

Of the Sick Brethren

B EFORE ALL THINGS AND above all things *care* is to be 15 Mar.
had of the sick, that they be served in very deed as 15 July
14 Nov.
Christ Himself, for He hath said: "I was sick, and ye visited
Me." And, "What ye have done unto one of these little ones, ye have
done unto Me." And let the sick themselves remember that they are
served for the honor of God, and not grieve the brethren who serve
them by unnecessary demands. Yet must they be patiently borne with,
because from such as these is gained a more abundant reward. Let it be
therefore the Abbot's greatest care that they suffer no neglect. And let a
cell be set apart by itself for the sick brethren, and one who is God-
fearing, diligent, and careful, be appointed to serve them. Let the use of
baths be allowed to the sick as often as may be expedient; but to those
who are well, and especially to the young, let it be granted more seldom.
Let the use of flesh meat also be permitted to the sick and to those that
are very weakly, for their recovery: but when they are restored to health,
let all abstain from meat in the accustomed manner. The Abbot must
take all possible care that the sick be not neglected by the Cellarer or
servers: because whatever is done amiss by his disciples is laid to his
charge.

37

Of Old Men and Children

ALTHOUGH HUMAN NATURE is of itself drawn to feel pity for these two times of life, namely old age and infancy, yet the authority of the Rule should also provide for them. Let their weakness be always taken into account, and the strictness of the Rule respecting food be by no means kept in their regard; but let a kind consideration be shown for them, and let them eat before the regular hours.

16 Mar.
16 July
15 Nov.

38

Of the Weekly Reader

READING MUST NOT BE wanting while the brethren eat at table; nor let anyone who may chance to have taken up the book presume to read, but let him who is to read throughout the week begin upon the Sunday. After Mass and Communion, let him ask all to pray for him, that God may keep from him the spirit of pride. And let this verse be said thrice in the Oratory, he himself beginning it: "O LORD, Thou shalt open my lips, and my mouth shall declare Thy praise." And so, having received the blessing, let him enter on his reading. The greatest silence must be kept at table, so that no whispering may be heard there, nor any voice except that of him who readeth. And whatever is necessary for food or drink let the brethren so minister to each other, that no one need ask for anything: but should anything be wanted, let it be asked for by a sign rather than

17 Mar.
17 July
16 Nov.

by the voice. And let no one presume to put any questions there, either about the reading or about anything else, lest it should give occasion for talking: unless perchance the Superior should wish to say a few words for the edification of the brethren. Let the brother who is reader for the week take a little bread and wine before he begin to read, on account of the Holy Communion,* and lest it be hard for him to fast so long. Afterwards let him take his meal with the weekly cooks and other servers. The brethren are not to read or sing according to their order, but such only as may edify the hearers.

---

* *Mixtum . . . propter Communionem sanctam.* The *mixtum* here spoken of is, according to the best authority, a small portion of bread and wine, identical with the *biberes et panem* prescribed in chapter 35. St. Benedict allows it to the reader, before commencing his duty, for two distinct reasons: one, lest he might find his task too laborious, if undertaken fasting: the other, to prevent any inconvenience or involuntary irreverence which might be entailed by the effort of reading aloud a short time after communicating. The most ancient commentators are unanimous in this interpretation of the words *propter Communionem sanctum;* and the *Regula Magistri*, which was written, according to Mabillon (*De Studiis monasticis*, II. 13), as early as the 7th century, and is in great part an amplification of the Rule of St. Benedict, has this direction for the reader: "Ipse suum merum *propter sputum sacramenti* accipiat, et tunc incipiat legere." Connected with this custom, of course, are the ablutions prescribed in the celebration of Mass, and also the practice, still observed in many places, of giving to the faithful a little wine or water immediately after Communion.

Perez sees in this expression of St. Benedict evidence that the practice of daily Communion prevailed in the early monasteries; but the words are probably intended to apply only to the *dies solemniores*, which are expressly mentioned in the analogous case of the weekly servers (chapter 35).

39

Of the Measure of Food

W E THINK IT SUFFICIENT for the daily meal, whether at the sixth or the ninth hour, that there be at all seasons of the year two dishes of cooked food, because of the weakness of different people; so that he who perchance cannot eat of the one, may make his meal of the other. Let two dishes, then, suffice for all the brethren; and if there be any fruit or young vegetables, let a third be added. Let one pound weight of bread suffice for the day, whether there be but one meal, or both dinner and supper. If they are to sup, let a third part of the pound be kept back by the Cellarer, and given to them for supper. If, however, their work chance to have been hard, it shall be in the Abbot's power, if he think fit, to make some addition, avoiding above everything, all surfeiting, that the monks be not overtaken by indigestion. For there is nothing so adverse to a Christian as gluttony, according to the words of our LORD: "See that your hearts be not overcharged with surfeiting." And let not the same quantity be allotted to children of tender years, but less than to their elders, moderation being observed in every case. Let everyone abstain altogether from the flesh of four-footed animals, except the very weak and the sick.

40

Of the Measure of Drink

E VERY ONE HATH HIS proper gift from God, one after this manner, another after that. And therefore it is with some misgiving that we appoint the measure of
other men's living. Yet considering the infirmity of the weak, we think that one pint of wine a day is sufficient for each: but let those to whom God gives the endurance of abstinence know that they shall have their proper reward. If, however the situation of the place, the work, or the heat of summer require more, let it be in the power of the Superior to grant it; taking care in everything that surfeit or drunkenness creep not in. And although we read that wine ought by no means to be the drink of monks, yet since in our times monks cannot be persuaded of this, let us at least agree not to drink to satiety, but sparingly: because "wine maketh even the wise to fall away." But where the necessity of the place alloweth not even the aforesaid measure, but much less, or none at all, let those who dwell there bless God and not murmur. This above all we admonish, that there be no murmuring among them.

41

At what Hours the Brethren are to take their Meals

F ROM HOLY EASTER until Pentecost let the brethren dine at the sixth hour, and sup in the evening. But
from Pentecost throughout the summer (unless they have to work in the fields or are harassed by excessive heat) let them fast on

Wednesdays and Fridays until the ninth hour, but on other days dine at the sixth. Should they have field labor, or should the heat of the summer be very great, they must always take their dinner at the sixth hour. Let the Abbot provide for this, and let him so arrange and dispose all things, that souls may be saved, and that the brethren may do what they have to do without just cause for murmuring. From the fourteenth of September until the beginning of Lent let them always dine at the ninth hour; and during Lent, until Easter, in the evening. And let the hour of the evening meal be so ordered that they have no need of a lamp while eating, but let all be over while it is yet daylight. At all times, whether of dinner or supper, let the hour be so arranged that everything be done by daylight.

42

That no one may Speak after Compline

MONKS SHOULD LOVE silence at all times, but especially during the hours of the night. Therefore, on all days, whether of fasting or otherwise, let them sit down all together as soon as they have risen from supper (if it be not a fast-day) and let one of them read the "Conferences" [of Cassian], or the lives of the Fathers, or something else which may edify the hearers. Not, however, Heptateuch, nor the Books of Kings: for it will not profit those of weak understanding to hear those parts of Scripture at that hour:* they may, however, be read at other times. If it be a fast-day, then

21 Mar.
21 July
20 Nov.

---

* *Infirmis intellectibus non erit utile.* The Heptateuch (or Books of Moses and Joshua) and the Books of the Kings would be considered too exciting to the imagination, to be suitable for reading immediately before retiring to rest. We read that Ulphilas, bishop of the Goths, omitted the Books of Kings in his translation of the Scriptures into the

a short time after Vespers let them assemble for the reading of the Conferences, as we have said; four or five pages being read, or as much as time alloweth, so that during the reading all may gather together, even those who may have been occupied in some work enjoined them. Everyone, then, being assembled, let them say Compline; and when that is finished, let none be allowed to speak to anyone. And if anyone be found to evade this rule of silence, let him be subjected to severe punishment; unless the presence of guests should make it necessary, or the Abbot should chance to give any command. Yet, even then, let it be done with the utmost gravity and moderation.

43

Of those who come Late to the Work of God, or to Table

AT THE HOUR of Divine Office, as soon as the signal is heard, let everyone, leaving whatever he had in hand, hasten to the Oratory with all speed, and yet with seriousness, so that no occasion be given for levity.

22 Mar.
22 July
21 Nov.

Let nothing, then, be preferred to the Work of God. And should anyone come to the Night-Office after the *Gloria* of the ninety-fourth Psalm (which for this reason we wish to be said very slowly and protractedly), let him not stand in his order in the choir, but last of all, or in the place set apart by the Abbot for the negligent, so that he may be seen by him and by all, until, the work of God being ended, he have made satisfaction by public penance. The reason why we have judged it fitting for them to stand in the last place, or apart, is that, being seen of all, they may amend for very shame. For, if they were to remain outside

---

vernacular, fearing lest the perusal of them might inflame the naturally war-like dispositions of his flock.

the Oratory, someone perchance would return to his place and go to sleep, or at all events would sit down outside, and give himself to idle talk, and thus an occasion would be given to the evil one. Let him therefore enter, that he may not lose the whole, and may amend for the future. At the day Hours, let him who cometh to the Work of God after the Verse,* and the *Gloria* of the first Psalm which followeth it, stand in the last place, as ordered above, and not presume to join with the choir in the Divine Office, until he hath made satisfaction: unless perchance, the Abbot shall permit him so to do, on condition, however, that he afterwards do penance.

If anyone, through his own negligence and fault, come not to table before the Verse, so that all may say this and the prayer together, and together sit down to table, let him 23 Mar. 23 July 22 Nov.
be once or twice corrected. If after this he do not amend let him not be admitted to share in the common table, but be separated from the companionship of all, and eat alone, his portion of wine being taken from him, until he hath made satisfaction and amends. Let him be punished in like manner, who is not present also at the Verse which is said after meals. And let no one presume to take food or drink before or after the appointed hour: but should a brother be offered anything by the Superior, and refuse to take it, if he afterwards desire either what be before refused, or anything else, he shall receive nothing whatever, until he hath made proper satisfaction.

---

* *i.e.*, Deus in adjutorium meum intende.

44

Those who are Excommunicated, how they are to Make Satisfaction

LET HIM, WHO FOR graver offences is excommunicated from the Oratory and the table, prostrate himself at the door of the Oratory, saying nothing, at the hour when the Work of God is being performed: lying prone, with his face upon the ground, at the feet of all who go out from the Oratory. Let him continue to do this until the Abbot judge that he hath made satisfaction; and then, coming at the Abbot's bidding, let him cast himself at his feet and at the feet of all, that they may pray for him. After this, if the Abbot so order, let him be received back into the choir, in such a place as he shall appoint: yet so, that he presume not to intone Psalm or lesson, or anything else, in the Oratory, unless the Abbot again command him. And at all the Hours, when the Work of God is ended, let him cast himself on the ground, in the place where he standeth, and so make satisfaction, until such time as the Abbot bid him cease therefrom. But let those, who for lighter faults are excommunicated only from the table, make satisfaction in the Oratory so long as the Abbot shall command, and continue so doing until he bless them and say it is enough.

24 Mar.
24 July
23 Nov.

45

Of those who make Mistakes in the Oratory

IF ANY ONE MAKE a mistake in the recitation of Psalm, responsory, antiphon, or lesson, and do not humble

25 Mar.
25 July
24 Nov.

himself by making satisfaction there before all, let him be subjected to severer punishment, as one who would not correct by humility what he did wrong through negligence. But children for such faults are to be whipt.*

46

Of those who Offend in any other Matters

I F ANY ONE, WHILE at work in the kitchen or the cellar, in serving the brethren, in the bake-house or the garden, or at any other occupation or in any place whatever, commit any fault, or break or lose anything, or transgress in any other way, and does not come immediately before the Abbot and community, and of himself confess and make satisfaction for his fault; if it is made known by another, he shall be subjected to more severe correction. If, however, the guilt of his offense be hidden in his own soul, let him manifest it to the Abbot only, or to his spiritual seniors, who know how to heal their own wounds, and will not disclose or publish those of others.

---

* *Infantes . . . vapulent.* The *infantes* or *pueri* referred to here and elsewhere in the Holy Rule were not boys receiving their education in the Monastery in view of some secular career, but were the *alumni*, properly so-called, or youthful aspirants to religious life, who wore the habit, and assisted at the Divine Office and other monastic exercises. The following passage from the *Ordo Cluniacensis* of Bernard, drawn up in the 11th century, curiously illustrates the fidelity with which the instructions of St. Benedict were carried out in mediaeval times.

"Ad Nocturnes, imo ad omnes Horas, si quid ipsi pueri offendunt in Psalmodia, vel in alio cantu, minime differtur: absque mora frocco et cuculla exuti judicantur, et in sola camisia caeduntur (nisi laici sint in ecclesia, a quibus videri possint): et hoc fit a Priore, vel eorum magistro, virgis vimineis levibus et teretibus, ad hoc provisis."

47

Of Signifying the Hour for the Work of God

LET THE ANNOUNCING of the hour for the Work of God, both by day and night, be the Abbot's care: either by signifying it himself, or by entrusting the duty to such a careful brother, that all things may be done at the appointed times. Let the Psalms and antiphons be intoned by those whose duty it is, each in his order, after the Abbot. Let no one presume to sing or to read except such as can so perform the office that the hearers may be edified. And let it be done with humility, gravity, and awe, and by those whom the Abbot hath appointed.

27 Mar.
27 July
26 Nov.

48

Of the Daily Manual Labor

IDLENESS IS AN ENEMY to the soul; and hence at certain seasons the brethren ought to occupy themselves in the labor of their hands, and at others in holy reading. We think, therefore, that the times for each may be disposed as follows: from Easter to the first of October, let them, in going from Prime in the morning, labor at whatever is required of them until about the fourth hour. From the fourth hour until near the sixth let them apply themselves to reading. And when they rise from table, after the sixth hour, let them rest on their beds in perfect silence; or if anyone perchance desire to read, let him do so in such a way as not to disturb anyone else. Let None be said in good time, at about the middle of the

28 Mar.
28 July
27 Nov.

eighth hour; and then let them again work at whatever has to be done, until Vespers. And if the needs of the place, or their poverty, oblige them to labor themselves at gathering in the crops, let them not be saddened thereat; because then are they truly monks, when they live by the labor of their hands, as did our fathers and the Apostles. Yet let all be done with moderation, on account of the fainthearted.

From the first of October to the beginning of Lent, let them apply to reading until the end of the second hour. Let Tierce be then said, and until the ninth hour let all labor at 29 Mar. 29 July 28 Nov. the work that is enjoined them. When the first signal for None is given, let everyone break off from his work, and be ready as soon as the second signal is sounded. After their meal, let them occupy themselves in their reading, or in learning the Psalms. During Lent, let them apply themselves to reading from morning until the end of the third hour, and then, until the end of the tenth, labor at whatever is enjoined them. And in these days of Lent let each one receive a book from the library, and read it all through in order. These books are to be given out at the beginning of Lent. Above all, let one or two seniors be appointed to go round the Monastery, at the hours when the brethren are engaged in reading, and see that there be no slothful brother giving himself to idleness or to foolish talk, and not applying himself to his reading, so that he is thus not only useless to himself, but a distraction to others. If such a one be found (which God forbid) let him be corrected once and a second time; and if he does not amend, let him be subjected to the chastisement of the Rule, so that the rest may be afraid. And let not one brother associate with another at unseasonable hours.

On Sunday, let all occupy themselves in reading, except those who have been appointed to the various offices. But if anyone should be so negligent and slothful, 30 Mar. 30 July 29 Nov. as to be either unwilling or unable to study or to read, let some task be given him to do, that he be not idle. To brethren who are weak or delicate, let there be given such work or occupation as to prevent them either from being idle, or from being so oppressed by excessive labor as to be driven away. Their weakness must be taken into account by the Abbot.

49

Of the Observance of Lent

ALTHOUGH THE LIFE of a monk ought at all times to have about it a Lenten character, yet since few have strength enough for this, we exhort all, at least during the days of Lent, to keep themselves in all purity of life, and to wash away, during that holy season, the negligences of other times. This we shall worthily do, if we refrain from all sin, and give ourselves to prayer with tears, to holy reading, compunction of heart and abstinence. In these days, then, let us add something to our wonted service; as private prayers, and abstinence from food and drink, so that every one of his own will may offer to God, with joy of the Holy Spirit, something beyond the measure appointed him: withholding from his body somewhat of his food, drink, and sleep, refraining from talking and mirth, and awaiting Holy Easter with the joy of spiritual longing. Let each one, however, make known to his Abbot what he offereth, and let it be done with his blessing and permission: because what is done without leave of the spiritual father shall be imputed to presumption and vain-glory, and merit no reward. Everything, therefore, is to be done with the approval of the Abbot.

31 Mar.
31 July
30 Nov.

50

Of the Brethren who are Working at a Distance from the Oratory, or are on a Journey

L ET THE BRETHREN who are at work at a great distance, or on a journey, and cannot come to the Oratory at the proper time (the Abbot judging such to be the case) perform the Work of God there where they are laboring, in godly fear, and on bended knees. In like manner, let not those who are sent on a journey allow the appointed Hours to pass by; but, as far as they can, observe them by themselves, and not neglect to fulfill their obligation of divine service.

1 Apr.
1 Aug
1 Dec.

51

Of the Brethren who go not very far off

L ET NOT THE BROTHER who is sent out on any business, and hopeth to return that same day to the Monastery, presume to eat while abroad, even although pressed by anyone to do so, unless perchance he have been bidden by his Abbot. If he do otherwise, let him be excommunicated.

2 Apr.
2 Aug
2 Dec.

52

Of the Oratory of the Monastery

ET THE ORATORY BE what it is called, a place of 　3 Apr.
prayer: and let nothing else be done, or kept there.* 　3 Aug
When the Work of God is ended, let all go out with the 　3 Dec.
utmost silence, paying due reverence to God, so that a brother, who
perchance wishes to pray by himself, may not be hindered by another's
misconduct. If anyone desire to pray in private, let him go in quietly and
pray, not with a loud voice, but with tears and fervor of heart. And let it
not be permitted, as we have said, to remain in the Oratory when the
Work of God is finished, except it be for a like purpose, lest hindrance
be caused to others.

53

Of Receiving Guests

ET ALL GUESTS THAT come be received like Christ 　4 Apr.
Himself, for He will say: "I was a stranger and ye 　4 Aug
took Me in." And let fitting honor be shown to all, 　4 Dec.
especially to such as are of the household of the faith, and to strangers.
When, therefore, a guest is announced, let him be met by the Superior
or the brethren, with all due charity. Let them first pray together, and

---

* *Geratur aut condatur.* The meaning is clear, although somewhat elliptically expressed.
Nothing was to be done in the Oratory, and nothing kept there *(condatnr)*, except what
pertained to the due celebration of the Divine Service.

thus associate with one another in peace; but the kiss of peace must not be offered until after prayer, on account of the delusions of the devil. In this salutation let all humility be shown. At the arrival or departure of all guests, let Christ—who indeed is received in their persons—be adored in them, by bowing the head or even prostrating on the ground.

When the guests have been received, let them be led to prayer, and then let the Superior, or any one he may appoint, sit with them. The law of God is to be read before the guest for his edification; and afterwards let all kindness be shown him. The Superior may break his fast for sake of the guest, unless it happens to be a principal fast-day, which may not be broken. The brethren, however, shall observe their accustomed fasting. Let the Abbot pour water on the hands of the guests; and himself, as well as the whole community, wash their feet; after which let them say this verse: "We have received Thy mercy, O God, in the midst of Thy Temple." Let special care be taken in the reception of the poor and of strangers, because in them Christ is more truly welcomed. For the very fear men have of the rich procures them honor.

Let the kitchen for the Abbot and guests be apart by itself; so that strangers, who are never wanting in a monastery, may not disturb the brethren by coming at 5 Apr.
5 Aug
5 Dec. unlocked-for hours. Let two brothers, who are well able to fulfill the duty, be placed in this kitchen for a year; and let help be afforded them as they require it, so that they may serve without murmuring. When they have not much to occupy them there, let them go forth to other work, wherever they may be bidden. And not only with regard to them, but in all the offices of the Monastery, let there be such consideration shown, that when there is need of help it may be given them; and that when they are without work, they do whatever they are commanded. Let the care of the guest-house, also, be entrusted to a brother whose soul is possessed with the fear of God: let there be sufficient beds prepared there and let the house of God be wisely governed by prudent men. Let no one, except he be bidden, on any account associate or converse with the guests. But if he chance to meet or to see them, after humbly

saluting them, as we have said, and asking their blessing,* let him pass on, saying that he is not permitted to talk with a guest.

54

Whether a Monk ought to Receive Letters or Tokens

B Y NO MEANS LET a monk be allowed to receive,   6 Apr.
either from his parents or anyone else, or from his   6 Aug
brethren, letters, tokens,† or any gifts whatsoever, or to give   6 Dec.
them to others, without permission of the Abbot. And if anything be sent to him, even by his parents, let him not presume to receive it until it hath been made known to the Abbot. But even if the Abbot order it to be received, it shall be in his power to bid it be given to whom he

---

* *Petita benedictione.* That is, after respectfully saluting the guest. *Benedicite* was the ordinary form of greeting.

† *Eulogias. Benedictiones.* This word is used by ancient writers, both in its Greek and Latin form, in the sense of "gifts" or "presents." Thus in 1 Kings 25:27, Abigail, referring to the presents she is offering to David, says: "Wherefore, receive this blessing which thy handmaid hath brought to thee." The word, as used here by St. Benedict, may bear the same meaning; but it is generally understood in the stricter ecclesiastical sense of the bread or small cakes which were blessed during Mass, and given to the faithful in token of their being in full communion with the Church. The *Eulogia* is still given in parts of France, and also in the Greek Church, where it is known by the name of ἀντίδωρον, as being a kind of substitute for Holy Communion. It was a monastic custom of the highest antiquity that these *eulogiæ*, or blest cakes, should be distributed to the brethren in the refectory, before beginning their meal. The *Capitula Monachorum Augiensium (circ.* A.D. 813) prescribe as follows: "In refectorio, data benedictione, veniant duo presbyteri ad Abbatem, et dant ipsi eulogium cæteris fratribus." So in the *Capitulare Aquisgranense* (A.D. 816), cap. lxvii. "Ut eulogiæ Fratribus a presbyteris in refectorio dentur." Cf. *Regula Magistri*, c. 76.

The object of the prohibition laid down by St. Benedict is of course to discourage particular friendships, or marks of individual affection, as opposed to the spirit of community life.

pleaseth; and let not the brother to whom it may have been sent be grieved, lest occasion be given to the devil. Should anyone, however, presume to act otherwise, let him be subjected to the discipline of the Rule.

55

Of the Clothes and Shoes of the Brethren

L ET CLOTHING BE GIVEN to the brethren suitable to the nature and the climate of the place where they live: for in cold countries more is required, in warm countries less. This must therefore be considered by the Abbot. We think, however, that in temperate climates a cowl and a tunic should suffice for each monk: the cowl to be of thick stuff in winter, but in summer something worn or thin: likewise a scapular for work, and shoes and stockings to cover their feet. And let not the monks complain of the color or coarseness of these things, but let them be such as can be got in the country where they live, or can be bought most cheaply.

Let the Abbot be careful about the size of the garments, that they be not too short for those who wear them, but of the proper length. When they receive new clothes let them always give up the old ones at once, to be put by in the wardrobe for the poor. For it is sufficient for a monk to have two tunics and two cowls for wearing at night, and also for washing: whatever is over and above this is superfluous, and ought to be cut off. In the same way, let them give up their shoes, and whatever else is worn out, when they receive new ones. Let those who are sent on a journey receive drawers from the wardrobe, and on their return restore them washed. Their cowls and tunics also, which are to be a little better than those they ordinarily wear, let them receive from the wardrobe when setting out on their journey, and give them back on their return.

For their bedding let a straw mattress, blanket, coverlet, and pillow suffice. These beds must be frequently inspected by the Abbot, to see if any private property be *8 Apr.* *8 Aug* *8 Dec.* discovered therein. And if anyone should be found to have anything which he hath not received from the Abbot, let him be subjected to the most severe discipline. In order that this vice of private ownership may be rooted out entirely, let the Abbot supply them with all necessaries: that is, a cowl, tunic, shoes, stockings, girdle, knife, pen, needle, handkerchief, and tablets; so that all plea of wanting anything may be taken away. Yet let the Abbot always be mindful of those words of the Acts of the Apostles: "Distribution was made to any one, according as he had need." Let him, therefore, consider the infirmities of such as are in want, and not the ill-will of the envious. Nevertheless, in all his judgments, let him think of the retribution of God.

56

Of the Abbot's Table

LET THE TABLE OF the Abbot be always with the guests and strangers. But as often as there are few *9 Apr.* *9 Aug* *9 Dec.* guests, it shall be in his power to invite any of the brethren. Let him take care, however, always to leave one or two seniors with the brethren for the sake of discipline.

57

Of the Artificers of the Monastery

S HOULD THERE BE artificers in the Monastery, let them
work at their crafts in all humility, if the Abbot gives
permission. But if any of them be puffed up by reason of
his knowledge of his craft, in that he seemeth to confer some benefit on
the Monastery, let such a one be taken from it, and not exercise it again,
unless, perchance, when he hath humbled himself, the Abbot bid him
work at it anew. And if any of the work of the artificers is to be sold, let
those by whom the business is done see that they defraud not the
Monastery. Let them ever be mindful of Ananias and Saphira, lest
perchance, they, and all who deal fraudulently with the goods of the
Monastery, should suffer in their souls the death which these incurred in
the body. But with regard to the prices of such things, let not the vice of
avarice creep in, but let them always be sold a little cheaper than by men
in the world, that God may be glorified in all things.

10 Apr.
10 Aug
10 Dec.

58

Of the Discipline of Receiving Brethren into Religion

T O HIM THAT NEWLY cometh to change his life, let
not an easy entrance be granted, but, as the Apostle
saith, "Try the spirits if they be of God." If, therefore, he
that cometh persevere in knocking, and after four or five days seem
patiently to endure the wrongs done to him and the difficulty made
about his coming in, and to persist in his petition, let entrance be

11 Apr.
11 Aug
11 Dec.

granted him, and let him be in the guest-house for a few days. Afterwards let him go into the Novitiate, where he is to meditate and study, to take his meals and to sleep. Let a senior, one who is skilled in gaining souls, be appointed over him to watch him with the utmost care, and to see whether he is truly seeking God, and is fervent in the Work of God, in obedience and in humiliations. Let all the hard and rugged paths by which we walk towards God be set before him. And if he promise steadfastly to persevere, after the lapse of two months let this Rule be read through to him, with these words: "Behold the law, under which thou desirest to fight. If thou canst observe it, enter in; if thou canst not, freely depart." If he still stand firm, let him be taken back to the aforesaid cell of the Novices, and again tried with all patience. And, after a space of six months, let the Rule be again read to him, that he may know unto what he cometh. Should he still persevere, after four months let the same Rule be read to him once more. And if, having well considered within himself, he promise to keep it in all things, and to observe everything that is commanded him, then let him be received into the community, knowing that he is now bound by the law of the Rule, so that from that day forward he cannot depart from the Monastery, nor shake from off his neck the yoke of the Rule, which after such prolonged deliberation he was free either to refuse or to accept.

Let him who is to be received make before all, in the Oratory, a promise of *stability, conversion of life,* and *obedience,* in the presence of God and of His saints, so that, if he 12 Apr.
12 Aug
12 Dec. should ever act otherwise, he may know that he will be condemned by Him whom he mocketh. Let him draw up this promise in writing, in the name of the saints whose relics are in the altar, and of the Abbot there present. And let him write it with his own hand; or at least, if he knoweth not how, let another write it at his request, and let the Novice put his mark to it, and place it with his own hand earn upon the altar. When he hath done this, let the Novice himself immediately begin this verse: "Uphold me, O LORD, according to Thy Word, and I shall live: and let me not be confounded in my expectation." And this verse let the

whole community thrice repeat, adding thereto *Gloria Patri*. Then let the newly-received brother cast himself at the feet of all, that they may pray for him, and from that day let him be counted as one of the community. Whatever property he hath let him first bestow upon the poor, or by a solemn deed of gift make over to the Monastery, keeping nothing of it all for himself, as knowing that from that day forward he will have no power even over his own body. Forthwith, therefore, in the Oratory, let him be stripped of his own garments, wherewith he is clad, and be clothed in those of the Monastery. And let the garments that are taken from him be laid by and kept in the wardrobe; so that if ever, by the persuasion of the devil, he consent (which God forbid) to leave the Monastery, he may be stripped of the monastic habit and cast forth. But the form of his profession, which the Abbot took from the altar, shall not be given back to him, but be kept in the Monastery.

59

Of the Sons of Nobles, or of Poor Men, that are Offered

IF ANY NOBLEMAN SHALL perchance offer his son to God in the Monastery, let the parents, should the boy be still in infancy, make for him the written promise as aforesaid; and together with the oblation* let them wrap that promise and the hand of the child in the altar-cloth, and so offer him up. With

13 Apr.
13 Aug
13 Dec.

---

* *Cum oblatione.* An offering, that is, of bread and wine, which was made by the parents at the offertory of the Mass in which their child was dedicated to God. (*Statuta Lanfranci*, c. 18; *Ordo Cluniacensis*, c. 27.) Mere infants were sometimes offered in this way; but most of the ancient monastic constitutions forbade them to be received before they had attained the age of reason, and could distinguish right from wrong. The ratification of the parents' act was conditional on the subsequent consent of the child, whose final and solemn consecration to religion could not take place until his fifteenth year. The Council of Trent afterwards (Sess. XXV., cap. 15) fixed the age for profession

respect to his property, they must in the same document promise under oath that they will never either themselves, or through anyone else, or in any way whatever, give him anything, or the means of having anything. Or else, if they are unwilling to do this, and desire to offer something as an alms to the Monastery, for their own advantage, let them make a donation of whatever they please to the Monastery, reserving to themselves, if they will, the income thereof during their life. Thus let all possibility of expectation be excluded whereby the child might be deceived and so perish (which God forbid), as we have learnt by experience may happen. Let those who are poorer do in like manner. But those who have nothing whatever may simply make the promise in writing, and with the oblation, offer their son before witnesses.

60

Of Priests who may wish to Dwell in the Monastery

I F ANYONE IN PRIESTLY orders ask to be received into the Monastery, let not consent be too quickly granted him; but if he persist in his request, let him know that he will have to observe all the discipline of the Rule, and that nothing will be relaxed in his favor, according as it is written: "Friend, wherefore art

14 Apr.
14 Aug
14 Dec.

---

at sixteen years complete; and Pius IX, by a decree promulgated in 1857, further ordained that simple vows only should be taken at the end of the novitiate, and that the final and crowning act of solemn profession should not take place until three years more had elapsed.

The *Ordo Cluniacensis* of Bernard, already cited, contains (cap. 17) a detailed account of the discipline and mode of education of these *alnmni*, or youthful monks, in one of the most important mediæval monasteries. The writer concludes his account with the expression of his opinion that "it is hard to see how a king's son could be brought up with greater care in a palace than the youngest boy receives in the Abbey of Cluny." (From the *Vetus Disciplina Monastica*, Paris, 1726.)

thou come?" Let him, nevertheless, be allowed to stand next the Abbot, to give the blessing, and to say Mass, if the Abbot bid him do so. Otherwise, let him presume to do nothing, knowing that he is subject to the discipline of the Rule; but rather let him give an example of humility to all. And if there be a question of any appointment, or other business in the Monastery, let him expect the position due to him according to the time of his entrance, and not that which was yielded to him out of reverence for the priesthood. If any clerics should desire in the same way to be admitted into the Monastery, let them be placed in a middle rank: but in their case also, only on condition that they promise observance of the Rule, and stability therein.

61

Of Stranger Monks, how they are to be Received

IF ANY MONK WHO is a stranger comes from distant parts, and desire to dwell in the Monastery as a guest, and if he be content with the customs which he there findeth, and do not trouble the Monastery by any superfluous wants, but be satisfied with what he findeth, let him be received for as long a time as he will. And if reasonably and with humility he reprove and point out what is amiss, let the Abbot prudently mark his words, in case God perchance hath sent him for this very end. If afterwards he desires to bind himself to remain there, let not his wish be denied him, especially since during the time he was a guest his manner of life could well be ascertained.

15 Apr.
15 Aug
15 Dec.

But if during that time he was found burdensome or prone to vice, not only must he not be admitted among the brethren, but he must even be courteously bidden to depart, lest others should be corrupted by his evil living. If, however, he

16 Apr.
16 Aug
16 Dec.

is not such as to deserve to be sent away, let him not merely on his own asking be received and admitted into the community, but even be persuaded to remain, that the others may be taught by his example: because in every place we serve one God, and fight under one King. And if the Abbot perceives him to be a man of this kind, he may put him in a somewhat higher place. It shall be in the Abbot's power to assign not only to a simple monk, but also to any of the aforesaid priests or clerics, a higher place than that due to them by their entrance into the Monastery, if he sees that their lives are such as to deserve it. But let the Abbot take care never to receive a monk from any known monastery, without his own Abbot's consent, and letters of recommendation; as it is written: "What thou wilt not have done to thyself, do not thou to another."

62

Of the Priests of the Monastery

IF ANY ABBOT DESIRES to have a priest or deacon ordained for his Monastery, let him choose from among his monks one who is worthy to fulfill the priestly office. And let him that is ordained beware of arrogance and pride, and presume to do nothing that is not commanded him by the Abbot, knowing that he is now all the more subject to regular discipline. Let him not, by reason of his priesthood, become forgetful of the obedience and discipline of the Rule, but advance ever more and more in godliness. Let him always keep the place due to him according to his entrance into the Monastery, except with regard to his office at the altar, or unless the choice of the community and the will of the Abbot should raise him to a higher place for the merit of his life. Nevertheless, let him know that he must observe the rules prescribed by the deans or provosts. Should he presume to do otherwise, he shall be judged, not as a priest, but as a rebel; and if after frequent warning he does not correct himself, let recourse be had to the intervention of the Bishop.* If even then he will not amend, and his guilt is clearly shown, let him be cast forth from the Monastery, provided his contumacy be such that he will not submit nor obey the Rule.

63

Of the Order of the Community

LET EVERYONE KEEP THAT place in the Monastery, which the time of his entering religion, the merit of his life, or the appointment of the Abbot shall determine. And let not the Abbot disquiet the flock committed to him, nor by an undue use of his authority ordain anything unjustly; but let him ever hear in mind that he will have to give an account to God of all his judgments and all his deeds. Therefore in that order which they hold, or which he shall have appointed, let the brethren receive the kiss of peace, approach to Communion, intone the Psalms, and stand in choir. And in no place whatsoever let age decide the order, or be prejudicial to it; for

18 Apr.
18 Aug
18 Dec.

---

* *Episcopus adhibeatur in testimonium.* These words are usually interpreted to mean that the Bishop was to be actually called upon to intervene in the case of a refractory priest. Taken in conjunction with the appeal to the Ordinary prescribed in the event of an improper election to the abbacy (chapter 64), they seem to show that St. Benedict did not, in laying down his Rule, contemplate that exemption from episcopal authority which his Order afterwards enjoyed. It has been maintained, indeed, that no trace of such exemption is to be found previous to the time of St. Gregory the Great (590-604). P. Bouix, however (*De jure Regularium*, 11., cap. 2. § 1), clearly shows that there were instances of this immunity, at least in the Eastern and African Churches, two centuries or more before the above date, and therefore considerably anterior to the time of St. Benedict.

Samuel and Daniel, when but children, judged the elders. Excepting, therefore, those whom (as we have said) the Abbot hath promoted with some special object, or for distinct reasons hath degraded, let all the rest stand in the order of their coming to religion; so that, for example, he who entered the Monastery at the second hour of the day must know that he is lower than he who came at the first hour, whatever may be his age or dignity. The children are to be kept under discipline at all times and by every one.

Let the younger brethren, then, reverence their elders, 19 Apr. and the elder love the younger. In calling each other by 19 Aug 19 Dec. name, let none address another by his simple name; but let the elders call the younger brethren *Brothers,* and the younger call their elders *Fathers,** by which is implied the reverence due to a father. But let the Abbot, since he is considered to represent the person of Christ, be called "Lord" and "Abbot," not that he hath taken it upon himself, but out of reverence and love for Christ. Let him be mindful of this, and show himself to be worthy of such an honor. Wherever the brethren meet one another, let the younger ask a blessing from the elder. And when the elder passeth by, let the younger rise, and give place to him to sit down; nor let the younger presume to sit with him, unless the elder bid him, that it may come to pass as it is written: "In honor preferring one another." Let young children and boys take their places in the Oratory, or at table, with all due discipline. In other places also,

---

* *Nonnos.* This designation continued for many centuries to be applied to the elder members of the monastic Community. Bernard of M. Cassino, in his commentary (of the end of the 13th century) speaks of *nonnus Remigius, nonnus Jacobus,* &c. The title of *Nonnus* was afterwards superseded (except among the Cistercians, who still retain it) by that of *Domnus,* of which indeed some have maintained it to be merely another form. The word is found in late Latin writers in the sense of "tutor" or "master." (Inscr. ap. Zaccaria, *Stor. lett. d' Italia,* tom ix., p. 492.) It is probably of Egyptian origin, and was applied in very early times to the monks and nuns of Egypt. (*Vid.* S. Jerome, Epist. 117, No. 6, and 22, No. 16. *Vitæ Patrum, passim,* &c.) It occurs frequently also in the African Church, as a proper name: we read of a St. Nonnus, an Abbot Nonnus, and others. The mother of St. Gregory Nazianzen was named Nonna. The word still survives in our "nun" (= nonna).

wherever they may be, let them be under proper care and discipline, until they come to the age of understanding.

64

Of the Appointment of the Abbot

IN THE APPOINTING OF an Abbot, let this principle always be observed, that he be made Abbot whom all the brethren with one consent in the fear of God, or even a small part of the community with more wholesome counsel, shall elect. Let him who is to be appointed be chosen for the merit of his life and the wisdom of his doctrine, even though he should be the last in order in the community. But if all the brethren with one accord (which God forbid) should elect a man willing to acquiesce in their evil habits, and these in some way come to the knowledge of the Bishop to whose diocese that place belongs, or of the Abbots or neighboring Christians, let them not suffer the consent of these wicked men to prevail, but appoint a worthy steward over the house of God, knowing that for this they shall receive a good reward, if they do it with a pure intention and for the love of God, as, on the other hand, they will sin if they neglect it.

20 Apr.
20 Aug
20 Dec.

Let him that hath been appointed Abbot always bear in mind what a burden he hath received, and to whom he will have to give an account of his stewardship; and let him know that it beseemeth him more to profit his brethren than to preside over them. He must, therefore, be learned in the Law of God, that he may know whence to bring forth new things and old: he must be chaste, sober, merciful, ever preferring mercy to justice, that he himself may obtain mercy. Let him hate sin, and love the brethren. And even in his corrections, let him act with prudence, and not go too far, lest while he seeketh too eagerly to scrape off the rust, the vessel be broken. Let him

21 Apr.
21 Aug
21 Dec.

keep his own frailty ever before his eyes, and remember that the bruised reed must not be broken. And by this we do not mean that he should suffer vices to grow up; but that prudently and with charity he should cut them off, in the way he shall see best for each, as we have already said; and let him study rather to be loved than feared. Let him not be violent nor over anxious, not exacting nor obstinate, not jealous nor prone to suspicion, or else he will never be at rest. In all his commands, whether concerning spiritual or temporal matters, let him be prudent and considerate. In the works which he imposeth, let him be discreet and moderate, bearing in mind the discretion of holy Jacob, when he said: "If I cause my flocks to be overdriven, they will all perish in one day." Taking, then, the testimonies borne by these and the like words to discretion, the mother of virtues, let him so temper all things, that the strong may have something to strive after, and the weak nothing at which to take alarm. And, especially, let him observe this present Rule in all things; so that, having faithfully fulfilled his stewardship, he may hear from the LORD what that good servant heard, who gave wheat to his fellow-servants in due season: "Amen, I say unto you, over all his goods shall he place him."

65

Of the Provost of the Monastery

I T HAPPENETH VERY often that by the appointment of the Provost grave scandals arise in Monasteries; since there are some who, puffed up by the evil spirit of pride, and deeming themselves to be second Abbots, take upon themselves to tyrannize over others, and so foster scandals and cause dissensions in the community: especially in those places where the Provost is appointed by the same Bishop, or the same Abbots as appoint the

22 Apr.
22 Aug
22 Dec.

Abbot himself. How foolish this custom is may easily be seen; for from his first entering upon office an incentive to pride is given to him, the thought suggesting itself that he is freed from the authority of his Abbot, since he hath been appointed by the very same persons. Hence are stirred up envy, quarrels, backbiting, dissensions, jealousy, and disorders. And while the Abbot and Provost are at variance with one another, it must needs be that souls are endangered by reason of their disagreement; and those who are their subjects, while favoring one side or the other, run to destruction. The evil of this peril falleth on the heads of those who by their action have been the cause of such disorders.

We foresee, therefore, that it is expedient for the preservation of peace and charity, that the ordering of the Monastery depend upon the will of the Abbot. If possible, 23 Apr.
23 Aug
23 Dec.
let all the affairs of the Monastery be attended to (as we have already arranged) by Deans, as the Abbot shall appoint; so that, the same office being shared by many, no one may become proud. But if the needs of the place require it, and the community ask for it reasonably and with humility, and the Abbot judge it expedient, let him himself appoint a Provost, whomsoever he shall choose with the counsel of brethren who fear God. Let the Provost reverently do whatever is enjoined him by his Abbot, and nothing against his will or command; for the more he is raised above the rest, so much the more carefully ought he to observe the precepts of the Rule. And if the Provost be found culpable or deceived by the haughtiness of pride, or be proved a contemner of the holy Rule, let him be admonished by words until the fourth time, and then let the correction of regular discipline be applied to him. But if even then he does not amend, let him be deposed from the office of Provost, and another, who is worthier, be substituted in his place. If afterwards he be not quiet and obedient in the community, let him be expelled from the Monastery. Nevertheless, let the Abbot bear in mind that he must give an account to God of all his judgments, lest perchance the flame of envy or jealousy be kindled in his soul.

66

Of the Porter of the Monastery

A T THE GATE OF the Monastery let there be placed a wise old man, who knoweth how to give and receive an answer, and whose ripeness of years suffereth him not to wander about. He ought to have his cell near the gate, so that they who some may always find someone at hand to give them an answer. As soon as any one shall knock, or a poor man call to him, let him answer, "Thanks be to God," or bid God bless him, and then with all mildness and the fear of God let him give reply without delay, in the fervor of charity. If the porter needs help, let him have with him one of the younger brethren.

The Monastery, however, ought if possible to be so constituted that all things necessary, such as water, a mill, and a garden, and the various crafts may be contained within it; so that there may be no need for the monks to go abroad, for this is by no means expedient for their souls. And we wish this rule to be frequently read in the community, that none of the brethren may excuse himself on the plea of ignorance.

67

Of Brethren who are Sent on a Journey

L ET THE BRETHREN WHO are about to be sent on a journey commend themselves to the prayers of all the brethren and of the Abbot, and at the last prayer of the Work of God let a commemoration be always made of the absent. Let the brethren that return from a journey, on the very day that they come back, lie prostrate on the floor of the Oratory at all the Canonical Hours, while the Work of God is being performed, and beg the prayers of all on account of their transgressions, in case they should perchance upon the way have seen or heard anything harmful, or fallen into idle talk. And let no one presume to relate to another what he may have seen or heard outside the Monastery; for thence arise manifold evils. If anyone shall so presume, let him be subjected to the punishment prescribed by the Rule. And he shall undergo a like penalty, who dareth to leave the enclosure of the Monastery, or to go anywhere, or do anything, however trifling, without permission of the Abbot.

68

If a Brother be Commanded to do Impossibilities

I F ON ANY BROTHER there be laid commands that are hard and impossible, let him receive the orders of him who biddeth him with all mildness and obedience. But if he seeth the weight of the burden altogether to exceed his strength, let him seasonably and with patience lay before his Superior the reasons of his incapacity to obey, without showing pride, resistance, or contradiction. If, however, after this the Superior still persists in his command, let the younger know that it is expedient for him; and let him obey for the love of God, trusting in His assistance.

26 Apr.
26 Aug
26 Dec.

69

That no one Presume to Defend another in the Monastery

CARE MUST BE TAKEN that on no occasion one monk presume to defend another in the Monastery, or to take his part, even although they be connected by some near tie of kinship. Let not the monks dare to do this in any way whatsoever because therefrom may arise the most grievous occasion of scandals. If anyone transgress this rule, let him be very severely punished.

27 Apr.
27 Aug
27 Dec.

70

That no one Presume to Strike another

LET EVERY OCCASION OF presumption be banished from the Monastery. We ordain, therefore, that no one be allowed to excommunicate or strike any of his brethren, unless authority to do so shall have been given him by the Abbot. Let such as offend herein be rebuked in the presence of all, that the rest may be struck with fear. With regard to the children, however, let them be kept by all under diligent and watchful discipline, until their fifteenth year: yet this, too, with measure and discretion. For if anyone presume, without leave of the Abbot, to chastise such as are above that age, or show undue severity even to the children, he shall be subjected to the discipline of the Rule, because it is written: "What thou wouldest not have done to thyself, do not thou to another."

28 Apr.
28 Aug
28 Dec.

71

That the Brethren be Obedient one to the other

NOT ONLY IS THE excellence of obedience to be shown by all to the Abbot, but the brethren must also obey one another, knowing that by this path of obedience they shall come unto God. The commands, then, of the Abbot or the Superiors appointed by him (to which we allow no private orders to be preferred) having the first place, let all the younger brethren obey their elders with all charity and vigilance. And should anyone be found refractory, let him be corrected. But if a brother be rebuked by the Abbot, or any of his Superiors, for the slightest cause, or if he perceive that the mind of any Superior is even slightly angered or moved against him, however little, let him at once, without delay, cast himself on the ground at his feet, and there remain doing penance until that feeling be appeased, and he giveth him the blessing. If anyone should disdain to do this, let him either be subjected to corporal chastisement, or, if he remain obdurate, let him be expelled from the Monastery.

29 Apr.
29 Aug
29 Dec.

72

Of the Good Zeal which Monks ought to have

AS THERE IS AN evil zeal of bitterness, which separateth from God, and leads to hell, so there is a good zeal, which keepeth us from vice, and leadeth to God and to life everlasting. Let monks, therefore, exert this zeal with most fervent love; that is, "in honor preferring one another." Let them most

30 Apr.
30 Aug
30 Dec.

patiently endure one another's infirmities, whether of body or of mind. Let them vie with one another in obedience. Let no one follow what he thinketh good for himself, but rather what seemeth good for another. Let them cherish fraternal charity with chaste love, fear God, love their Abbot with sincere and humble affection, and prefer nothing whatever to Christ. And may He bring us all alike to life everlasting.

73

That the Whole Observance of Perfection is not Set down in this Rule

WE HAVE WRITTEN THIS *Rule,* in order that, by observing it in Monasteries, we may show ourselves to have some degree of goodness of life, and a beginning of holiness. But for him who would hasten to the perfection of religion, there are the teachings of the holy Fathers, the following whereof bringeth a man to the height of perfection. For what page or what word is there in the divinely inspired books of the Old and New Testaments that is not a most unerring rule for human life? Or what book of the holy Catholic Fathers doth not loudly proclaim how we may by a straight course reach our Creator? Moreover, the *Conferences of the Fathers,* their *Institutes* and their *Lives,* and the Rule of our holy Father Basil— what are these but the instruments whereby well-living and obedient monks attain to virtue? But to us, who are slothful and negligent and of evil lives, they are cause for shame and confusion. Whoever, therefore, thou art that hasteneth to thy heavenly country, fulfill by the help of Christ this least of Rules which we have written for beginners; and then at length thou shalt arrive, under God's protection, at the lofty summits of doctrine and virtue of which we have spoken above.

1 May
31 Aug
31 Dec.

For additional titles from

Ichthus Publications

visit our website at

www.ichthuspublications.com

34196603R00052

Made in the USA
Middletown, DE
11 August 2016